The Student Entrepreneur's Guide

How To Start And Run Your Own Part Time Small Business

By Brett Kingstone

TEN SPEED PRESS

Ten Speed Press
PO Box 7123
Berkeley, California 94707

Library of Congress Catalog Number 81-50251
ISBN: 0-89815-045-0

Book design and production by FIFTH STREET DESIGN ASSOCIATES

Photograph on front cover by Chuck Painter. Courtesy of Stanford
University News and Publications Service. Upper right photograph on
back cover by Rick Browne. Lower left photograph on back cover by
Michael Guttentag.

Illustrations of Dupie on pages 24, 56, 74 and 96, and cartoon on page 70
Copyright © 1981 Gil Morales, The Dupie Press.

Student Entrepreneur Quiz and Entrepreneurial Quiz on pages 70-71
reprinted from VENTURE, The Magazine for Entrepreneurs, by special
permission. © 1981 Venture Magazine, Inc., 35 West 45th Street,
New York, NY 10036.

Chart on page 143 reprinted from the December, 1979 issue of VENTURE,
The Magazine for Entrepreneurs, by special permission. © 1979 Venture
Magazine, Inc., 35 West 45th Street, New York, NY 10036.

10   9   8   7   6   5   4   3   2   1

To

MAX O. KINGSTONE
1888–1978

Businessman, Inventor, Entrepreneur

An Independent Man

Contents

LIST OF FIGURES / page 7

FOREWORD / page 9

PREFACE / page 11

SECTION ONE / page 13

The Spirit of American Free Enterprise

SECTION TWO / page 23

Business Ideas

SECTION THREE / page 55

General Planning

Researching the business. Researching the market. Analyzing time and money. Partnerships. Kingstone Bedding Warehouse. Small business management. Weighing advantages and disadvantages. Are you an entrepreneur?

SECTION FOUR / page 73

Getting Started

The business plan. Licenses and permits: state seller's permit, employer registration, fictitious business name statement, zoning permits, business licenses. Federal identification numbers: social security, employer identification. Attending to details. Pricing. Advertising. Hiring help. Insurance. Copyrights and patents. Incorporating.

SECTION FIVE / page 95

Administering the Business

Record keeping and accounting: bank accounts, ledgers. Taxes: sales tax, federal income tax, self-employment tax, estimated income tax, tax deductions, state income taxes, payroll taxes.

SECTION SIX / page 139

Entrepreneurial Studies

University of Southern California. Baylor University. Carnegie-Mellon University. Getting credits.

APPENDIX A / page 149

SBA Management Assistance Publications

APPENDIX B / page 151

Procedures for Opening Businesses in New York City

BIBLIOGRAPHY/page 157

List of Figures

Figure 1 – Time Chart/page 60

Figure 2 – Score Fact Sheet/page 65

Figure 3 – Executive Volunteer Corps Flyer/page 66

Figure 4 – Seller's Permit/page 78

Figure 5 – Application for Seller's Permit/page 79

Figure 6 – Fictitious Business Name Statement/page 81

Figure 7 – Proof of Publication for "DBA"/page 82

Figure 8 – City Zoning Clearance/page 84

Figure 9 – City Business License/page 84

Figure 10 – Form SS-5 Social Security Number/page 85

Figure 11 – Form SS-4 Federal Employer ID Number/page 86

Figure 12 – Sales Receipt with Sales Agreement and Check for Down Payment/page 98

Figure 13 – Invoice for Shipment Received/page 99

Figure 14 – Invoice for Delivery Made/page 100

Figure 15 – Rental Agreement/page 101

Figure 16 – Business Check/page 102

Figure 17 – Bank-Depositor Agreement/page 103, 104

Figure 18 – Expenditure Ledger/page 106, 107

Figure 19 – Income Ledger/page 108

Figure 20 – State Sales Tax Return/page 110, 111

Figure 21 – Business Tax Structure Chart/page 114

Figure 22 – Schedule C Profit (Loss) Statement (Sole Proprietorship)/page 116, 117

Figure 23 – Form 1065 Partnership Return of Income/page 118

Figure 24 – Form 1040 Individual Income Tax Return/page 121, 122

Figure 25 – Schedule SE Social Security Self-Employment Tax/page 123

Figure 26 – Form 1040-ES Federal Estimated Tax Worksheet/page 124

Figure 27 – Form 540 California Income Tax Return/page 128, 129

Figure 28 – Schedule C California Profit (Loss) Statement/page 130, 131

Figure 29 – California Estimated Tax Worksheet/page 132

Figure 30 – Payroll Chart/page 133

Figure 31 – W-4 Employee's Withholding Allowance Certificate/page 134

Figure 32 – Form 941 Employers Quarterly Federal Tax Return/page 135

Figure 33 – Form 940 Employers Annual Federal Unemployment Tax Return /page 136

Figure 34 – W-2 and W-3 Wage and Tax Statements/page 137

Figure 35 – Graduate Courses for Entrepreneurs/page 143

Figure 36 – SCIRE Project Application/page 146

FOREWORD

As a university professor of some years, I always hope that my teaching efforts might spark at least a handful of young men and women into taking up a career in business management or accounting. In the case of Brett Kingstone, that spark kindled the spirit of American free enterprise. Fully charged, Brett's keen desire was to become a student entrepreneur.

Not willing to wait for graduation, Brett Kingstone succeeded in putting together a fairly sophisticated and profitable small business enterprise. This book attests to that.

The material summarizes the author's experiences over approximately a nine-month period beginning January 1980. However, it is not just a personal statement. As a well known talk show co-host would say: "This book contains everything you'd want to know about student entrepreneurship." Well, almost. Certainly, it covers many planning, administrative, legal and marketing aspects of small business management. With an introductory accounting course and good common sense, all budding student entrepreneurs should find the material lively and interesting reading.

Working on this report was satisfying indeed. I observed an accounting student transform himself into an intelligent business manager. Brett, the future is yours.

Paul A. Griffin
Assistant Professor
Stanford University
Graduate School of Business
September 1980

PREFACE

You can become an entrepreneur! The purpose of this book is to show you how. Many students have started their own businesses while in college. These students are the type who refuse to wait and let all their good ideas pass by. Student entrepreneurs prefer to profit from their ideas now. Becoming an entrepreneur will give you a tremendous amount of practical business experience that will enhance your present studies as well as your future career. Tired of boring theoretical economics classes? Sick of working as a part-time photocopier, food server, or book checker? Then stop plodding along in your mundane chores, do something really profitable and exciting: become your own boss! I promise you it will be one of the best investments you will ever make as a student.

This book is a basic "how to" guide for students who are interested in starting their own part-time small businesses. But it can also serve as a useful reference book for housewives and full time employees who are interested in starting and operating a small business in their spare time. The initial chapters on student business ideas from all over the country will make exciting and interesting reading for people of all ages and professions. In the following pages, I will present many unique ideas that have blossomed into student run enterprises and show you all the steps you must take in order to start a new enterprise of your own.

Much of this book is based on my own experiences as a student entrepreneur. During my junior year at Stanford University I established and operated a small business of my own, the Kingstone Bedding Warehouse. I decided to go into business mainly because I was bored stiff with theoretical economics classes and wanted to do something practical. I was tired of hearing about it—I wanted to see if I could *do* it. I kept the business small, deliberately, and closed it down when my "experiment" was over and academic credit had been granted. The experience I gained even in that short time was invaluable, but what I found most exhilarating was the challenge and competition, the excitement of making a sale, the satisfaction of seeing profits start to grow. There's nothing like being your own boss!

I was able to use this venture as a research project, for which I received five units of academic credit. Part of the project requirement was to write a paper on my experience and on the research I had done in connection with it, and that is how this book got its start. To add more background to it, I spent a good deal of time interviewing student entrepreneurs all over the country. I was amazed at the number of students who are operating their own businesses, amazed at the many creative ideas they have, and at how successful many of them have been. I decided to include a lot of the interview material in this book, so the *Student Entrepreneur's Guide* is more than a how-to book. It also portrays what I consider to be a new wave of entrepreneurism that is taking place on college campuses today.

This book was written under the guidance of Professor Paul Griffin of the Stanford Graduate School of Business. Professor Griffin was the faculty sponsor for my business project and has always provided me with an abundance of thought, insight, and ideas for both my business and this book. His interest and enthusiasm was unending and it has been a privilege to study under him.

I would also like to thank Professor Robert Davis for advising me on the marketing of my business and the production of this book. Every time I left Professor Davis' office, I wanted to go out and conquer the world. Need I say more about his motivating qualities?

Paula Davidson and Jackie Wan have been a tremendous help in typing and editing this book. They have taken my jumbled scrawlings and miraculously converted them into readable English.

I will always be grateful to Mrs. Anita Alcabes who was my DECA advisor (Distributive Education Clubs of America) in high school for she took a rather wild young man with a tremendous amount of energy and gave him direction and purpose.

I would also like to thank my parents, Renee and Leonard Kingstone, whose advice, support, and love have been a tremendously motivating force in my life. This book is dedicated to my grandfather, Max O. Kingstone, who came to this country as a penniless young boy and built up an independent family business that has enabled all his grandsons to go to college. His whole life has been an example which my brothers and I intend to follow.

Brett Kingstone
Stanford, 1980

The Spirit of American Free Enterprise

There is a spirit still alive in America today. Far from dead, as so many people may think, it burns bright in the hearts of many Americans. I am speaking of the spirit of American free enterprise. This spirit is sparked by individual ambition and self-confidence, and is fostered by the freedom of choice we enjoy in this country and the opportunity we have to go as far as that ambition and hard work will take us. This spirit is what has made our country great from colonial times up to the present and I believe it is our hope for the future.

Many pessimists feel that the current economic decline has spelled doom for both the free enterprise system and for the bold venturers anxious to strike out on their own. But I feel as long as this country operates under the free enterprise system, and as long as there are people with competitive spirit and the desire for success, new ideas will be developed into successful businesses.

Enterprising Americans have played a major role in the development of our country, and I have often looked to their life stories for inspiration. In my opinion, the finest example of true entrepreneurship lies in the story of two ambitious students from Stanford who started a small business in a garage workshop many years ago. Their little venture has since grown to be a multi-million dollar corporation. I want to tell you a little more about them in the hopes that their story will be a source of inspiration for you, too.

These two students met during their undergraduate years at Stanford, where they were both enrolled in the electrical engineering department. The two friends wanted to start a small electronics business as soon as they graduated, and discussed their plans with Professor Fred Terman. Terman was a brilliant teacher, but more than that, he was a friend and trusted advisor. He saw great ability in these two students, and had confidence in their future success. However, he felt that the time was not right, (it was early in the 1930's—the field of electronics was in its infancy, and the country was recovering from the depression) and suggested they get a little more experience first.

15

So the two parted, one to work for General Electric in their research department, the other to do graduate work at MIT.

Three years later, the two returned to Stanford more determined than ever to start their own business. They set up a small workshop in a garage and began experimenting with and building various electronic devices, selling enough to keep themselves solvent, squeezing in worktime between classes and study (they were both enrolled in graduate school at Stanford.) Their inventions were wide-ranging, to say the least—everything from electronic harmonica tuners to audio oscillators. Terman recalls that in the first years of the company's development, he was able to tell how the business was doing by driving by their house. If the car was parked outside, it meant that business was good—they were busy at work and needed all the garage space to work on their equipment. If there was no car, it meant that they were not at work and business was slow.

For two years they struggled along. Then, in 1938, the Walt Disney studios bought nine pieces of equipment from them to use in the sound production for "Fantasia," and the company was on its way. From a two-man garage workshop operation it has grown into a corporation that employs 57,000 people and in 1980 had sales of $3.1 billion. It manufactures more than 4,000 different products, and its operations are now worldwide. The names of the two men who founded and built this industrial empire, in case you haven't already guessed, are William Hewlett and David Packard.

Their story has long been an inspiration to me, living proof of what individuals can accomplish on their own in the American free enterprise system. Hewlett and Packard started their business in 1939, but I know that the age of entrepreneurship is far from over. In fact I believe that it has been reborn. My conversations with student entrepreneurs all over the country have convinced me that the political pendulum has swung back to the basic ideals of free enterprise and that there is now a whole new generation of Hewletts and Packards who will create the innovations in products and services which will rejuvenate our economy.

Brett Johnson, a Harvard junior majoring in economics, is one of them. Brett began with a very simple idea—printed *caps* instead of printed T-shirts. The idea came to him during his freshman year when he was making a little money hawking T-shirts at the Harvard-Yale football game. He got his business venture into operation, and by the next Harvard game was ready to sell his caps, white painter's caps with a red "H" silk-screened on the front of each one.

Convinced that his idea had great potential, he took a year off from

Clockwise from top left: The small garage where Hewlett and Packard started their business; Packard and Hewlett (seated) test their first big success, the 200 A audio oscillator;

HP's first instrumentation computer, developed in 1966; a 1972 innovation, the HP-35 scientific calculator; Bill Hewlett, Fred Terman (standing) and David Packard.

school in order to concentrate on marketing his caps. He took on a full-time business partner, Bradley Peterson, who was a recent graduate from the University of Minnesota. The two entrepreneurs aggressively marketed their "crowd caps" and successfully landed contracts with the ROTC promotional campaign, Pepsi Cola promotional campaign, the Barry Manilow concert tour, and, of course, with the Harvard Athletic Department, to name just a few. They've been selling their caps in numbers well over 200,000. Last year Crowd-Caps Corporation grossed over $250,000 and is expected to gross over $1 million next year.

———————

Roger Conner is another bold entrepreneur, a real modern-day Horatio Alger hero who started as an unpaid worker in a small flower shop and became the owner of a florist company whose sales are well over $100,000 a year. His story is proof that the age-old combination of rugged individualism, hard work and free enterprise is as strong and as effective as ever. And he did it all before reaching the age of twenty.

One day, when he was only twelve, Roger stopped at a local flower shop and asked the owner if he could work for him, without pay, in order to learn the business. Roger started working there every day after school and part-time on Saturdays. After two years on the job, he finally asked for a small salary. The owners told him he "wasn't good enough to be paid"—so he quit, and found a paying job at another local flower shop. He worked hard there, but after six months the flower shop laid him off because business was slow.

Undaunted, Roger decided to go it alone and start his own flower store in the basement of his home. At the age of fifteen he started his business with only $65. He bought old refrigerators at garage sales and knocked the shelves out in order to turn them into coolers to house his fresh-cut flowers. His business grew rapidly as he built up a reputation for top quality, fine service, and a pleasant personality.

In August of 1977, Roger bought out the flower store where he had worked without pay for over two years. The people who said "he wasn't good enough" were astonished to find that they were being taken over by a teenager who had plans to renovate their whole store. In fact, one of the reasons why the owners sold to Roger was that their store was not doing well. After Roger took over ownership and renovated the store, business started booming. In fact, business was so good that after one year, Roger said he celebrated his first anniversary by buying the other flower store where he had worked. Roger is now planning to consolidate his operation by moving to a new downtown location which will have 2,000 square feet and seven employees.

FLOWERS BY ROGER

Roger Conner
4514 Central Avenue   October 20, 19??
Middletown, Ohio

Dear Roger:

I would like to take this opportunity on behalf of
Governor Ronald Reagan and myself to thank you so
very, very much for all the valuable time and effort
you have contributed in making the luncheon a success.

We are most grateful to you for this memorable day.

Sincerely,

Senator Donald "Buz" Lukens

Governor Ronald Reagan

*Roger Conner and his shops.
When he was fifteen he handled
the floral arrangements for a town
banquet for Governor Reagan.
In November of 1980 Roger was
selected as one of five florists
to be considered for the floral
display at the inauguration.*

Brent Pennington, a Baylor student, is one of those special people who not only invented something but perfected it, produced it, and is now distributing it. He designed an improved safety cut-off switch for central air-conditioning systems which he calls Safe-T-Stat. It is a small 5 × 3 × 3-inch switch—a heat-sensitive link in the switch breaks at 165 degrees so that, if there is a fire, the air-conditioning system will cut off. This will save lives by preventing smoke and flames from being spread through a house or office by the air conditioner. To date, he has sold over 2,000 of his units to wholesale electrical distributors in the Dallas-Fort Worth area and he plans to expand his distribution throughout the state of Texas, then nationally.

Pennington comes by his interest in electrical work quite naturally. His father owns a small electrical company, and he'd worked there since he was a teenager. In fact, he manufactured the first Safe-T-Stats on a small drill press set up in the back of his father's electrical shop. When orders started increasing, he hired someone to assist him with the drilling and assembly. He manages to produce and market his product in-between attending classes and on weekends.

Brent Pennington works on his
Saf-T-Stat; an ad for his invention

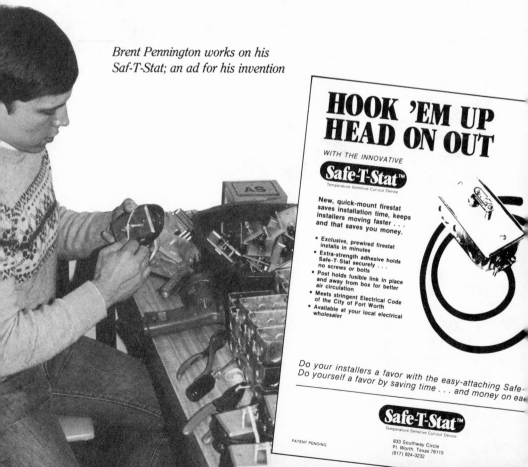

HOOK 'EM UP HEAD ON OUT

WITH THE INNOVATIVE

Safe-T-Stat™
Temperature Sensitive Cut-out Device

New, quick-mount firestat saves installation time, keeps installers moving faster . . . and that saves you money.

- Exclusive, prewired firestat installs in minutes
- Extra-strength adhesive holds Safe-T-Stat securely . . . no screws or bolts
- Post holds fusible link in place and away from box for better air circulation
- Meets stringent Electrical Code of the City of Fort Worth
- Available at your local electrical wholesaler

Do your installers a favor with the easy-attaching Safe-
Do yourself a favor by saving time . . . and money on ea

Safe-T-Stat™
Temperature Sensitive Cut-out Device

PATENT PENDING   833 Southway Circle
Ft. Worth, Texas 76115
(817) 924-3232

And there are many other young dynamos, some of whom you will meet later in this book, people like Steve Wilson who invented the Analog Input/Output Converter, Chris Fontana and Debbie Laster who own a restaurant called Munchies, Debbie Weiss who started as a fashion consultant and now heads a nationally-known firm called Darron Weiss Swimwear.

These entrepreneurs refuse to accept hyper-inflation and a declining standard of living as something we must all learn to accept. As long as the human mind has creativity, ideas can come forth to make our lives more fruitful, healthy, and productive. My discussions with student entrepreneurs all over the country have proven to me that I am not alone in my belief in a bright future for America.

During the past ten years, there has been a dramatic change in the attitudes of our nation's youth. The pendulum has definitely swung back to the basic ideals of the free enterprise system. If you take a closer look at our nations' youth today you will find the incurable optimists, the doers, the believers, the men and women who I believe will lead our country and build our future.

Brett Johnson and "friends" showing off their Crowd Caps.

Business Ideas

You are probably thinking to yourself that there's no way you fit into this grand picture I've been painting. But you do! No matter how small your venture (and as long as you are a student, you *should* keep it small) you will still be part of this exciting movement. Keep in mind that 95 percent of American businesses are classified as *small* businesses. Besides, if you check into the history of any large corporation, you'll probably find it had very humble beginnings. Remember Hewlett and Packard? They started out in their garage with not much more than a drill press, screwdriver, file, soldering iron, and hacksaw.

As I said before, all it takes is a good idea, and the ambition to do something with that idea. So now, let's discuss that all-important item, the business idea, the better mousetrap or super service that will be the basis of your new venture. It could be almost anything. Successful student-run businesses run the gamut from chocolate-chip cookies to computer systems, from rock bands to real-estate management. Some were started with $20 or $25 worth of supplies; others required large capital investment for stock or equipment. Some require only a few hours per day of one person's time; others may have dozens of employees. Some operate out of a dorm room; others require store or warehouse space.

The possibilities and variations are infinite, but to be practical, your range of choices should be narrowed to fit your needs. Not every venture will suit your knowledge or interests, your financial resources, or your time limitations. In your quest for that perfect business idea, you may reject many before finding that golden opportunity. But don't be impatient—time spent on this phase of entrepreneurship will be well worth it!

This section, I hope, will stimulate your creativity by presenting you with a wealth of ideas which student entrepreneurs all over the country have turned into successful businesses. I also hope that you will pick up some of their keys to success so you can apply them to your own venture. I believe that I have learned more about business from interviewing entrepreneurs for this book than in all my academic studies and research combined. If you can learn by reading about other people's successes and failures, you'll be one step ahead of the game, too, and will be better able to analyze your own activities. For many, this section may be the most important part of the book.

One of the schools I visited was Babson College in Wellesley, Massachusetts. Babson's Center for Entrepreneurial Studies, under the guidance of Dr. John A. Hornaday, offers an excellent program of courses, seminars, continuing education classes, research projects and student meetings with successful entrepreneurs. What makes the Babson program unique is that it encourages students to practice what they learn. As a result, there are probably more student entrepreneurs at Babson than on any other college campus in the United States.

Here is a sampling of some of the businesses at Babson. Many are very simple ideas that could work successfully on almost any campus and would require very little investment. One of these may work for you.

Babson Dry Cleaning

Babson Dry Cleaning is currently run by Eric Rahn. The business pools the cleaning orders of students all over campus and contracts the work out to a local cleaner. The business saves students money by offering lower group cleaning rates. The overhead is low because the business essentially serves as a "middleman" operation.

Babson Tire Sales

Babson Tire Sales is Babson College's oldest student business. It was started by Mark Babson (no relation, I checked it out) in 1953. Babson Tire Sales provides tires and auto parts at great money saving discounts to the Babson community.

Campus Student Services

John Demerill and Phil O'Flarety run Campus Student Services which rents refrigerators to students throughout the Boston area. Refrigerator rentals are very popular among college students across the country. It enables them to keep perishable food in their dorms so they can have early morning and late night snacks, or beers, on hand when the studies keep them up late. The refrigerator rental service is very well subscribed and employs three students each year.

Continental Promotions Co.

Continental Promotions, which is run by F. Thomas Godart, has introduced a new advertising publication called Godart's Product Mart, which will allow national advertisers to reach the college market through guaranteed distribution. Godart has distributed his publication to over 40,000 college students who live in the Boston area in a test market situation. If Godart's innovative distribution methods prove to be successful, he plans on making the publication go nationwide.

Custom Bumper Stickers

Jeff Mulligan is the creative entrepreneur who established Custom Bumper Stickers in 1979. Mulligan's company specializes in the small quantity message market. However, recently the company has moved into retail sales by printing large quantities of popular messages and selling them through local stores. The company has acquired two presses and has had a first year return of investment of 73 percent. Not bad!

Donahue-Burke Advertising

Donahue-Burke has been publishing an annual "Student Savings Booklet" for the past four years. This booklet offers discounts to students from local merchants. Donahue-Burke also publishes tourist guides and road maps and they are currently looking into expanding their market throughout the Boston area. Discount books and tourist and sports guides are common student enterprises. Jim and John Bear do it at Stanford, Curt Feldman does it at the University of Michigan as do Greg Hesterberg, Dave De Varti, and Tim Kunin of Sport Guides, Inc. If there is no such thing in your area, you might want to try it yourself.

E.Z.2.C.

E.Z.2.C., run by John Wadman, offers a unique advertising gimmick for businesses wishing to get their message to Babson students. The company employs the use of a rear projection screen located in Babson's dining hall. Advertisements are mixed with pictures of students and events to draw attention to the 4×5-foot screen.

Kustom Kakes of Wellesley

Kustom Kakes of Wellesley, run by Nina A. Depasquale and Janet C. Kalustian, offers parents and students of the Babson community a special delivery service of birthday and all-occasion cakes. All cakes are made to order and delivered directly from one of the local bakeries. This is an excellent business idea which can be used on any college campus.

Meyer Productions

Carl Meyer, president of Meyer Productions, deals in customized large volume orders of bumper stickers printed on vinyl. He also provides entertainment for private parties and local restaurants.

Moor Painting Co.

Moor Painting Company specializes in house painting for residents in the surrounding Babson communities. The company, run by Richard Carlson and Anthony Marken, gives free estimates and offers high quality house painting at a reasonable cost.

Plant Emporium

The Plant Emporium, run by John Dutton, offers plant sales, and "babysitting" for plants during vacation periods, plant rentals, repotting and plant doctor advice. The babysitting service was extended to Wellesley and Pine Manor Colleges and he has prepared the way for future plant sales there.

Publications Unlimited

Jonathan Carson got his Publications Unlimited venture off the ground by publishing programs for the Babson College Soccer Team. Carson is now publishing the soccer programs for the Ivy League and Yankee League Conferences and during the winter season he will publish hockey programs for the small New England colleges.

Ross-Galvin and Company

Michael Galvin and Duncan Ross founded Ross-Galvin and Company in 1975. Their company grew from a small town gardening service to a full service landscaping firm in just a few years. Ross-Galvin also engages in landscape design and construction, tree work, and snow removal. Last year, sales increased by more than 100 percent over the previous year.

Spring Breakaway

Tom Lydon's newly established Breakaway offers college students package trips to Bermuda and Florida during spring vacation breaks at reduced group rates.

Squash Unlimited

Squash Unlimited, run by Scot Banholzer and Kent Godfrey, specializes in offering the highest quality squash equipment on campus at the lowest prices. Because they keep a low overhead they are able to pass their savings on to the consumer.

Winter Wear

Winter Wear promotes pure wool, hand knit sweaters and down-filled vests to Babson students. The business success has led owners Jamie Adams and Tod Wellman to plan on expanding operations to neighboring college campuses.

World News Service

World News Service represents both the *New York Times* and the *Boston Globe* on the Babson campus. Mickey Rivers' aggressive marketing has enabled the company's sales to jump 250 percent.

As you can see, most of these enterprises require little initial expense and no specialized knowledge, and can be adjusted easily to fit almost any school schedule. A little organization, a little work, and a little advertising to let people know what services are being provided, or what goods offered for sale, and you're in business. Here are a few similar business ideas:

Magnetic Transfer

Bill Pielemeier, a student at the University of Michigan, Ann Arbor, has a business called Magnetic Transfer. He buys huge lots of high quality blank cassette tapes from a cassette duplication studio. By buying in large volume he can sell his tapes at half the price of comparable quality name-brand tapes.

Pielemeier markets his product by placing advertisements in dorms. His ads have his home phone number listed and he has an answering machine hooked up to his phone when he is away so that he never misses calls. He only sells his tapes in amounts of a dozen or more which cuts down on time and money spent in making deliveries. He mails an introductory sales package to new customers who want to try out his tapes. The packet contains sales literature and one sample tape. If the customers like the tape, they can send him the payment in a self-addressed return envelope which is provided in the packet. Otherwise, they return the tape.

After the new customers have received the introductory packet Pielemeier will call them, give a sales pitch, and ask if they are interested in ordering in a quantity of a dozen or more. He discounts his tapes to $1.85 each for an order of 25 or more, $1.70 for an order of 100 or more, and $1.55 each for an order of 250 or more. After the initial order, Pielemeier will deliver the tapes directly to the student. His experience has shown that these large quantity discounts encourage students living in a dormitory to pool their orders thus giving him one big order at the highest possible discount. He feels this marketing strategy not only saves him time in delivery trips, but also encourages students to get their friends to buy from him.

Pielemeier said his main concern in operating his own part-time business while at college was to limit the amount of time and overhead costs that his business would require. Bill has no store; he operates right out of his apartment. His advertising costs are very small because he designs his own ads and places them directly in the student dorms. He points out that many big businesses' advertising and overhead costs account for up to 50 percent of the price of the product and thus the customer comes out behind. Pielemeier claims that there is an unlimited market for shrewd entrepreneurs who start small businesses which offer products at prices below the large national competition. Staying small gives entrepreneurs a price advantage which allows them to compete very successfully with the big firms in their local sales area.

Baylor Balloons

Baylor seniors Karen Adams and Linda Knekow recently started a company called Baylor Balloons which specializes in delivering helium-filled balloons, $4 for a half-dozen, $8 for a dozen. They deliver by bicycle anywhere on campus at no extra charge. If a car is required for delivery, they charge an extra dollar. For party orders of five dozen or more, they give 10 percent discounts, and for orders of ten dozen or more, they give a 20 percent discount. So far, their business has made a big hit with birthday parties, sorority functions, anniversaries, congratulation gifts for people who have been accepted to medical school, etc.

When Adams and Knekow were considering starting a balloon business they contacted Professor Sexton of Baylor's entrepreneurship department in order to learn what would be required in terms of government registrations, and licenses. After obtaining the necessary licenses, the women proceeded to contact local merchants in order to find a store near campus which would rent them a small space. They soon found a tanning salon about half a block away from campus that agreed to rent them storage and counter space. Baylor Balloons thus went right into business. In fact, the business has been growing so fast that they will have to move into a record shop next door in a few weeks.

T & B Rock Impresarios

My good buddies, juniors Jamie Halper and Tim Quinlan, run T & B Associates, a booking agency for bands. According to Halper, T & B Associates books about half the bands that play on campus. The partners go to bars to hear bands play and audition them. (Note: Going to bars can be a tax deductible business expense!) They then set up engagements for the bands at campus dormitory and fraternity parties. For this service, T & B Associates charges $25 per booking, and this brings in about $500 per academic quarter. Halper and Quinlan say their business is fun and exciting in addition to being profitable.

Curt Feldman Enterprises

When he was a junior at the University of Michigan, Curt Feldman wrote a guide book to the Ann Arbor area. The book sold for about $3. When the initial printing of 1,000 was sold out, he ordered a second printing of 1,500; then a third printing of 3,000. Feldman also published a calendar which had pen and ink sketches of local restaurants on each page. His calendar sold for $4.95 and he sold out of his first printing of 1,400. Feldman claims his calendar's success was due to his practice of hiring student artists to do all his artwork. He says the students did the sketches for a reasonable price in order to have their work exposed and the buyers liked the idea that the calendar was entirely student made. Other Feldman enterprises are his Sunday morning *New York Times* and bagel delivery service to students and Ann Arbor residents and a University of Michigan Rose Bowl T-shirt. Incidentally, for those of you who don't know, the University of Michigan won the Rose Bowl last year.

The Men Behind The Money Book

In 1972, Jim Bear, then a senior, started a business which can be best described now as being somewhat of a Stanford tradition. Jim Bear's business was to develop and sell a coupon book which offers hundreds of dollars in discounts from local merchants to the Stanford community. During his senior year, Jim visited local merchants and sold enough of them on his idea to pay for his first press run. From 1972 to 1976 he sold over 3,000 copies a year. Jim was able to continue to operate his business at Stanford because after he graduated he went on to the Stanford Graduate School of Business and to the Law School.

Jim Bear displays his Money Book

Then in 1976 his brother John took it over. In just one year, John, who was then a sophomore at Stanford, expanded the book's sales from 3,000 to 7,500 by marketing the book all over the Palo Alto area in addition to the Stanford Campus. Net profits also jumped from $7,000 to $20,000 a year, and all this was for just 10 to 15 hours of work a week.

John Bear later expanded the business' line of products into athletic and entertainment guides, telephone directories, book covers and calendars. According to brother Jim, these businesses were always sure winners because they were relatively risk free, required low effort and a minimal capital investment. Essentially, John and Jim would contract advertising from local merchants for the money book and their other directories and pamphlets before the item would go to press. Thus the advertising alone would already have paid for the project. As far as the sales effort is concerned, most of their projects, once on the bookstore shelves, usually sell themselves because they design them to be unique and, especially in the case of the money book, worth much more than the cover price to the consumer.

The Pavement Sweeping Company

Scott Burns, a senior enrolled in Baylor's entrepreneurship program, started managing his own pavement sweeping company two years ago when he bought the operations of his uncle's company in the Waco area. Burns said he was interested in managing a company which he could operate at night so he could have his days free. He also was interested in managing his own company as a learning experience. When his uncle's Austin-based company was interested in selling its Waco operations, because the firm felt it had overexpanded and was becoming unmanageable, Burns jumped at the opportunity and bought it immediately. For $5,000, Burns acquired the rights to all the commercial contracts of the firm to do sweeping in the Waco area and a used truck which had a mechanized sweeper mounted on the back like a trailer. Burns did regular sweepings of parking lots and adjoining areas of retail stores and shopping centers.

You may not have $5,000 to invest in a sweeper, but smaller maintenance businesses don't require much investment, and, as Burns notes, it is easy to schedule your time in this business.

Roommate Match

At the University of Texas Pamela Douglas ran a roommate finding service out of her apartment. She kept extensive files on her clients so she could match people up by personality, desired location, hours, price level of rent, etc. She also tried to meet each person personally so that she could do a better job of finding compatible matches. A venture like this is relatively inexpensive to launch. You need to pay for an answering service or answering machine, and you need money for flyers and newspaper ads. After that, it's a matter of interviewing, filing, and phoning.

Hello Deli

Hello Deli is a late night food service run by Craig Foster, Brad Heinz, and Jonathan Slater, all students at Stanford. The partners purchase prepared sandwiches from a local deli every day. In the evening, they sell the sandwiches in the dorms to students who are suffering from the late night munchies. By selling directly, they know exactly what their customers want to eat, and they have a good idea how much to order. Thus we see a good example of on-the-job marketing research by the management.

Cookie Craze

The success of Hello Deli prompted Stanford senior Greg Warwick to start a late night cookie service dubbed Cookie Craze. Operating on the same order as Hello Deli, Greg buys big chocolate chip cookies from a local bakery and sells them, door-to-door, at the dorms all over campus. He buys the cookies for twenty-five cents each, and sells them for thirty-five cents. If he sells 600 cookies a night, he earns $60 for just a few hours work. Five nights a week would mean $300!

The Library Snack Bar

During the 1980 winter quarter, Kevin Wilson, another Stanford student, operated a snack bar in the evening in the undergraduate library lower lounge. Kevin's snack bar specialized in offering natural foods and juices, and was very popular with the students. It was in a convenient location and served as an alternative to the candy machines located just outside the library. Kevin opened his business as a project for a human biology class. After the class was completed he did not keep his business open due to other classwork demands, however, he believes that operating his own business during that one academic quarter was a "great experience" which was both interesting and profitable.

The Funk-a-Deli

At Harvard, Renee Reid, Diana Barcello, Tamy Lowe and Carol Brown manage the operations of the Funk-a-Deli which is located in a Harvard dormitory called Courier House. The Funk-a-Deli is a business that has been handed down over the last few years from student to student. Renee Reid claims they intend to provide the sandwiches and snacks which the students like best. She hopes by keeping in tune with her fellow students' tastes her business will thrive.

As long as there are hungry students, college campuses will continue to provide an excellent market for purveyors of food and drink. You can tap this market with almost anything from pickles to catered gourmet dinners, in anything from a wagon to a full scale restaurant, as long as you know who wants to eat what, and when and where to reach them. I have a friend who fires up a barbecue grill at lunch time and sells hot dogs near the Stanford student union. Simple! Of course, if you're going to open a restaurant, that's another story....

Munchies

Munchies is a small restaurant run by two Cornell University juniors who are in the School of Hotel Administration. Munchies serves hot sandwiches, pizza, deli products and home-baked goods. Since its opening, over 300 customers a day have been flocking to Munchies to dine on the delicious treats amidst a pleasant decor of hanging plants, quaint tables, and a well-kept hardwood floor.

Owners Chris Fontana and Debbie Laster had both had experience in restaurant work, and had decided they'd never get rich working for other people. So they went into business for themselves, and have done well enough to start thinking about opening a second restaurant. Their goal is to establish a chain of Munchies across the country.

Part of their success is due to creative promotions. They advertise in the local papers and on local radio stations, and have offered such special deals as a free *New York Times* with each order of quiche. During their first week of operation, they made up 5,000 pamphlets and hired a local high school track team to distribute them all over campus.

It was very interesting to learn how Fontana and Laster met and became friends. It seems that during their freshman year at Cornell they both had roommates who couldn't put up with them because they were both poor housekeepers and both liked loud music. As a result the roommates switched, and Fontana and Laster wound up together. Well, to make a long story short, they have been roommates ever since.

Chris Fontana and Debbie Laster take a Munchies break

I Can't Believe It's Yogurt

Another large scale food operation are the yogurt shops run by Bill Brice, a business student at SMU. His is not a typical story, but is still worth taking a look at. When Bill was a junior at Southern Methodist University he had a talk with the owner of two frozen yogurt shops in Dallas that were losing money and made him a deal: "You let me run the store for six months and bear the liability for any losses in exchange for the right to pocket any profits.... if after six months, I make the business profitable, you'll give me the option to buy you out." Well, Brice began managing the shop in January of 1978. He hired new employees, instituted strict cost controls, started an aggressive marketing campaign and was showing a healthy profit by June. So he obtained $30,000 from his savings and from loans and bought out both stores.

Today, twenty-three-year old Bill Brice has five "I Can't Believe It's Yogurt" shops in the Dallas area and he expects to have sixteen across the state of Texas by the end of 1983.

Brice is still attending Southern Methodist University on a part-time basis. He expects to obtain his Bachelors in Business Administration (BBA) in May of 1981. In the beginning, Brice spent from 80 to 100 hours a week managing his business so he didn't have the time to take a full course load. In the early months of his management, Brice didn't receive a salary; instead he reinvested any profits in the business in order to assure a strong growth and large future return. It seemed his strategy has worked. Last year Brice's business had gross sales of over $500,000 and he has received over a 35 percent return on his investment.

Brice felt that the yogurt shops had a good product but its failure, before he took over, was due to the fact it was poorly marketed and poorly managed. His secret to success was in hiring and motivating good employees and designing an attractive marketing campaign to advertise his product both on and off campus. Brice believes that if you have good employees working with you, your business will function as an efficient team. Apparently he's got a winning team!

Can you play a musical instrument? Are you artistic? Handy with tools? Can you speak a foreign language? If you have a special talent or expertise, with a little imagination, you could probably turn it into a profit-making business. Here are a few examples of businesses based on the special knowledge or skills of their proprietors:

Dynamic Sound

Jim Goldman, a senior at Cornell University, is the founder and president of Dynamic Sound, a company which handles the music and lighting for parties. Goldman started his company last year after working in a local disco as a disc jockey. When the disco closed he acquired some of their records and bought some equipment and started his own travelling disc jockey company for parties. Jim's business charges from $90 to $115 a night. He says at the typical party he conducts three-and-a-half hours of music and lighting. On an average he does about three jobs a month, and business picks up to about three parties a week during the weeks before Christmas and summer breaks.

Goldman's original partner left for MIT last semester so he got together with another partner, James T. Talcott, who is a sophomore majoring in electrical engineering. According to Goldman, "Talcott has an awesome pair of speakers," and thus the partnership was mutually beneficial. Together they purchased a set of amplifiers for $1,300 which have greatly enhanced their performances. They also took out an advertisement in the yellow pages and signed an advertising contract with the local newspaper, *The Cornell Daily Sun*.

DYNAMIC SOUND

Flexible arrangements to meet your needs. Dynamic Sound can provide the exact combination of price, equipment, and music that will take care of your social plans. For occasions of all types, our goal is to make your event the best it can possibly be. With our extensive record library, we specialize in a combination of Rock and Disco, but don't let that limit your imagination. Perhaps you have other ideas about the music for your party, something new and different or maybe old and reminiscent. Whatever—let us help you with the sound. Call us. Our system is something that we like to talk about.

Dynamic Sound . . . The name is new. Our company is young but is built upon years of experience in music and audio. Give us the opportunity to make the best in party music for your event.

Crown, Yamaha, Altec, Gauss . . . are just a few of the names, names that the professionals depend upon for sound. Quality equipment that is made for the road. 600 watts of total power output, 300 watts per channel to provide clean sound.

The price will surprise you. Talk to us so that we can make an estimate for your next affair. Call 257-5150 or 273-8039.

A flyer for Dynamic Sound

Rainbow Painters

Carl Rubo, senior at the University of Maryland, is the entrepreneur behind a painting and light construction company called Rainbow Painters. Carl first thought of the idea during the summer after his freshman year while he was working as a manager of a condominium in Ocean City, Maryland. At the time he was working there, the condominium was accepting bids from contractors to repaint the entire facility. Carl figured out that by hiring a few friends he could easily underbid the lowest bidder and do a high quality paint job at a pretty nice profit. The bid was accepted by the owner of the condominium and thus his business got under way.

Word got around about Carl's painting business and he was offered contracts with another condominium and a few restaurants in the Ocean City and Delaware area. Carl did most of the work during the summers and usually hired twelve people to do the work on a contract basis. During 1980 his business operated all year round and he hired three full-time workers. Carl was able to pay his workers from $200 to $250 a week depending on their efficiency and the amount of time spent with his firm. Carl says that he always offers opportunity for advancement. Those who exhibit leadership ability he appoints as crew chiefs who supervise the job site and rake in $300 a week. Not bad for a company predominantly made up of students!

While he is not directing his own operations, Carl's entrepreneurial energies are spent directing the campus operations of "Punch Poster" which he serves as the campus representative. Punch Poster is a business which sells posters geared for the college dormitory market. After graduation, Carl plans to take the next year off away from school to operate his business full time. After building up his clientele and selling off his business, Carl hopes to return to school to obtain a law degree.

The Soft Image

Another entrepreneur who is using his talents is Stanford sophomore David Gottfried. He operates The Soft Image, a portrait photography business. Gottfried just started his business this spring and invested $400 worth of personal funds to get it off the ground. He realizes that the nature of his business is very risky and competitive due to the great number of professional photographers available but he says, "I'm willing to fail and I'm willing to get nailed, simply because I want to learn." This statement in my mind shows the true goal and character of a successful student entrepreneur.

The first time I met David Gottfried, we happened to cross tracks in Professor Davis' office in the Graduate School of Business. It turned out that Professor Davis was serving as an advisor to both of us on our business projects. Our appointments were scheduled one right after the other, and after talking with each other about our businesses for a few minutes, we both decided to stay and have our advisory session together. The ideas and enthusiasm that were generated during that meeting were fantastic. We both learned a tremendous amount from each other. It is surprising how great a catalyst student entrepreneurs can be to one another when they start discussing their businesses and creative marketing, sales, and production ideas.

A good entrepreneur is quite willing to accept the challenge and take the risks in order to obtain the experience and the opportunity for profit. At the same time I spoke with Dave, his business was just in its first few weeks of operation and was going a bit slow but he hadn't lost a bit of enthusiasm or confidence. Dave strongly asserted that he is going to give his new business his best shot and if it doesn't work out he will find another idea which will. Again let me stress that ideas are available as fast as you can think of them, but it's your own self-confidence, determination, ambition, and enthusiasm which will make the good ideas become successful enterprises.

Pics-Gifts-Etc.

Baron Cook, an enterprising young finance and economics major at Baylor, also used his talents as a photographer to start his own company about three years ago. He began by taking pictures himself at sorority and fraternity parties. His photography service became so successful that he later hired other photographers to work for him. This past summer, Cook decided to branch out into selling fraternity and sorority clothes and personalized gifts in addition to his pictures. He rented a store across the street from campus and thus his business, Pics-Gifts-Etc, went into operation.

Cook currently has about eight photographers and three artists working for him. His artists design personalized lettering and fraternity emblems which he sews on clothing and has painted on gift items. His store is open from 12 noon to 6 pm Monday through Friday, and from 9 am to 12 noon on Saturday. This enables Baron to attend his classes in the morning. He also has one employee who works in the store during the day to help out with the customers and to take over when he has to run errands.

Cook went into these two ventures because there were no others like them in the area at that time. He had no competition for a ready market. His business sense was good—in two years, the number of groups he photographed quadrupled. As for the gift shop, it had sales of $55,000 in its first six months of operation.

Cook's business philosophy is "if you're going to go into business for yourself the best way to maximize your profit and minimize your costs is to do as much as you can by yourself." Cook buys large quantities of sweats directly from a manufacturer and sews the Greek letters on himself instead of buying them from a jobber, who sells the sweats presewn. He uses the same strategy in hiring his own artist to paint his customers' initials on his gifts. Cook also says there is no substitute for hard work. He says "My business was only able to make good money through my hard work." Cook will be graduating this June and he is contemplating selling his business so he may go on to other ventures. He says about four or five people have approached him with offers to buy his business.

Designer's Choice

During her years at the University of Maryland, Debbie Weiss ran a company called Designer's Choice, which specialized in reviewing people's wardrobes and making alterations to modernize their clothes. For men, Designer's Choice would coordinate shirts, ties and suits. For women, it would alter hemlines and restyle blouses and dresses. Most of Weiss' business came from the "Capitol Hill clientele." Her flair for fashion design was well-regarded enough that she could earn $40 an hour.

After she graduated with a degree in fashion design, Debbie was unable to find a job with any of the major fashion designers, so she decided to start her own company. Darron Weiss Swimwear, as the company is called, has done very well. The line is sold in many major department stores; last year 4,000 of the high-fashion swimsuits were sold, and this year she hopes to sell 10,000. Debbie is sole owner of the company, and handles all the selling, shipping, patterns, and designs. Debbie feels that her enthusiasm is probably the greatest asset of her company, a point we'd all do well to remember.

And what if you have no special talents and someone else has already cornered the cookie, sandwich, and every other market you can think of? Don't let that stop you. Plenty of business ideas are not much more than the product of a creative imagination and a sense of humor.

The Inflation Hedge

Stanford economics major Andy Newmark came up with a gimmick to beat the high cost of living. It is a spongy piece of green moss mounted on a wood block. A metal nameplate proclaims it "The Inflation Hedge." The hedge comes with its very own booklet, "The Care and Nurturance of Your Inflation Hedge," which was designed by Newmark's friend and business partner, Randy Schienberg. The hedge has had nationwide media coverage and sales have been great.

Andy Newmark and Randy Schienberg with a good supply of Inflation Hedges

Teddy Bear Tuck-In Service

Then there's the Teddy Bear Tuck-In Service (later called Pillow Talk, Inc.), the brainchild of University of Maryland student Herman Robinson. For a small fee, full tuck-in service is provided to any fair young campus coed—she is given a teddy bear to hold while two gentlemen in three-piece suits tuck her in, and another, clad in pajamas, reads her favorite bedtime story to her. Asked about the profitability of the enterprise, Dave West, a seasoned veteran of the service, said, "It's enabled us to keep a full beer keg in the dorm through the whole semester. What more could you want?" I guess by most college standards, that's all you could ask for.

Outcall Cheerleaders, Etc.

In Woodside, California, the high school cheerleading squad formed a company called Outcall Cheerleaders which delivers specially designed cheers at parties and other special occasions. "Cheer-O-Grams" have been sent to showers, birthday parties, office parties, and as general spiritlifters. In a similar vein, Diane Inabinett, at the University of Arizona, delivers personalized messages dressed up as Miss Piggy. She charges $20 to $30 per appearance, and averages five calls a week. I have also heard of dancing chocolate chip cookies and mime messengers.

Once in a while, someone comes up with a brand new idea or an improvement on existing designs that is absolutely revolutionary. The catch is that it takes more than just a brilliant idea... someone has to turn it into a marketable item, figure out how to produce it economically, and then get it out into the market place. For those who possess the combined talents of inventor and entrepreneur, the sky's the limit. Brent Pennington, whom you met earlier, is an example of the breed, as is Steve Wilson.

Data Acquisition Systems, Inc.

Steven Wilson, a junior at Harvard, is an inventor-entrepreneur par-excellence. He has designed a measuring device which can take information from a productive process and convert it into a message that can be read into a computer. His device is called the Analog Input/Output Converter. In April of 1980, Wilson along with Matthew Clark, Steve Brand and Mike Fridkin, all students at Harvard, established Data Acquisition Systems, Inc. (DAS) which was developed to manufacture and market this brave new device.

Michael Fridkin, Steven Wilson, Matthew Clark and Steven Brand of DAS

According to inventor Wilson, the DAS V Analog Input/Output system does much more than read information and transmit it to a computer. The device can also transcribe and transport messages from the computer to the process which is being regulated. This device has almost unlimited uses and application for both science and industry where computer regulation of a scientific or productive process is required. Seeing the opportunity for success for this device, Wilson and his associates invested $1,000 each, rented space in a small warehouse in Cambridge, Massachusetts, purchased the initial parts, and their new enterprise was off and running. During the past summer they all stayed at Harvard perfecting the device. Steve Wilson is currently taking a year off from school to assemble and market the product full time.

It is difficult to believe that Steve Wilson designed this unique device with almost no formal training in computer science or electronics. Steve basically taught himself electronics by assembling and repairing stereos, lamps, and TV sets. Wilson says he loves to "fiddle around" with electronics. His prowess in fiddling landed him a part-time job with the Harvard Bio Labs where he was inspired to build this device. All of Wilson's associates are majoring in areas outside the computer and electronics field.

What makes the company work is their creativity, perseverance and ambition.

The Analog Input/Output Converter is in its final design stage and has undergone trial production. By the time this book is published, Wilson expects to be in full production.

A small advertisement announcing their product in *Byte* and *Microcomputing Magazine* brought over 2,500 inquiries from the United States and Canada. Similar analog devices which can only be adapted to large computers are currently selling on the market for about $10,000 to $15,000. Wilson's device will list for $1,500 and can be adapted to small microcomputers selling for $1,500–$2,000 such as the Apple II Computer. Already a number of computer products distributors have asked to market the product.

Nike

People all over America are familiar with Nike running and athletic shoes, but how many know that the idea for Nike was conceived and planned as a project for a course at the Stanford School of Business. Phillip H. Knight, the president and co-founder of Nike, designed his business plan for the construction and marketing of his own line of athletic shoes in 1960 while studying at Stanford University's Graduate School of Business. Knight went into partnership in 1964 with William J. Bowermann, his former track coach at the University of Oregon. In 1972, the two began importing their own line of athletic shoes under the Nike name.

Nike, named for the Greek goddess of victory, has had a skyrocketing growth due to the jogging and athletic craze in the U.S. over the past years and Nike's innovative shoe design and aggressive marketing campaign. Nike has grown to be the largest supplier of higher quality athletic shoes in the U.S. and the third largest in the world. Sales were $269 million in 1980 and Mr. Knight expects sales for 1981 to top $430 million.

Knight was an avid runner as an undergraduate. He wanted to design and produce a lighter-weight running shoe and market it against the West German imports, Adidas and Pumas, and Japan's Tiger. After many interesting experiments designing soles with a waffle iron, Knight and Bowermann finally hit on a design that would be lighter and more comfortable and durable than all the other running shoes on the market. With advice from his old track coach and from many friendly athletes, Knight perfected the design. Soon Nike running shoes began showing up at major track meets, and students all over the country, runners and non-runners alike, were buying his shoes.

At many colleges and universities, the student government or an agency independent of the school may operate such businesses as bookstores, employment agencies, newsstands, etc. Most of these businesses would be impractical for the small business entrepreneur to consider, but some could be scaled down. In addition, it should be noted that operations of this sort fill many needs. Not only do they perform some necessary services, they also provide job opportunities for students, and practical training in business management for those who actually take part in running the agencies.

Harvard Student Agencies

Harvard Student Agencies run ten separate businesses: a linen service; a distribution service for posters, newspapers, and telegrams; an agency which manages a candystand, gameroom, and clean-up operation; a custodial service; an operation that sells rings and textbooks and leases TV sets, typewriters, fans, and refrigerators; a catering service; a travel agency; a bartending school; a temporary employment agency; and a publishing company.

According to HSA president Mark Battey, all the agencies are run on a non-profit basis. Last year seven out of the ten agencies had gross sales of over $100,000.

Cornell Student Agencies

Cornell Student Agencies (CSA) is probably the oldest student-run business conglomerate in the United States. It was founded in 1894 by a very high spirited entrepreneur by the name of Seth Higby who started out by carrying student laundry in a wheelbarrow to a local laundromat. Higby's laundry service became very popular and spread all over campus. Higby began hiring other students to run his operation and taught a few how to manage it so they could take over the operation when he graduated. As the business began to branch out into other ventures, shares in the company were sold to students in order to acquire additional capital. In 1910, the business was formally incorporated as an independent student-run corporation. Last year, Cornell Student Agencies had gross sales of over $700,000 and the projected fiscal 1981 gross sales are for $850,000.

Peter Nolan, the current president of Cornell Student Agencies, says that CSA has fourteen major agencies which employ an average of seventy workers a week. The agencies employ two full-time non-student consultants and one full-time secretary. All of the management positions of each

agency are staffed by Cornell students. According to Nolan the employees
receive an hourly wage and the managers of each agency are paid on a
profit-sharing basis. Nolan expects that this year three or more students
will receive at least $10,000 as their share of the agency's profits for the
year.

Some of the agencies run by CSA are: a "Homefinders" agency
which assists students in house and apartment hunting; a cap and gown
agency for graduation ceremonies; a college desk blotter agency; a refrigerator and fan rental service; a bus charter agency; a newsstand agency; a
birthday cake service which delivers birthday cakes to students at their
dorm; a carpet agency which sells carpet scraps to students for their dorms
or apartments; a summer storage service; a travel service desk which sells
Youth Hostel and Student ID cards; a campus novelty sales operation
which sells Cornell posters and pennants; a telephone directory advertising service; and, last but not least, a real estate management agency.

President Nolan asserts that CSA is entirely independent both
legally and financially of the University. It is not dependent on any outside
funding or donations. In fact, CSA has been so successful that it has been
making donations to the University's scholarship fund. Nolan points out
that because CSA is independent of the slow moving university bureau-
cracy, "we can move fast in making our own investment decisions, especially when we are confronted with new projects." In fact their reputation
for their efficiency in establishing new enterprises has led many local
banks and businesses to contact CSA when they desire to sell a business.
Nolan said that he has let the word out that he will entertain any offer for a
new business opportunity. Their recently established Homefinders
Agency was acquired from a local bank and their summer storage agency
was purchased from two Cornell students who were independently
operating their own storage agency for a number of years.

Nolan sees a great future ahead for Cornell Student Agencies. His
one regret is that the student management doesn't stay on long enough to
carry out all the long range plans. The officers are only allowed to stay on
for a period of one year. Nolan does believe that even during this short
period of time a tremendous amount is accomplished and the officers leave
with very valuable practical business experience.

Associated Students of Stanford University

In addition to having many private free lance entrepreneurs, Stanford also has some very well established enterprises which are run by the
student association. The Associated Students of Stanford University

(ASSU) manages student services such as: lecture notes, T-shirt printing, course guides and, until recently, "special events." The ASSU's annual budget for last year was over $1.5 million.

The lecture note service sells notes of the major lecture classes for a nominal fee. Often this service allows students to spend more time in class thinking about what the professor is saying and less time frantically trying to write down his every word. The ASSU also operates a T-shirt service which prints anything (well almost) on the T-shirt of your choice. The T-shirt service has been a big hit with dorms, frats, and intramural teams. Every quarter the ASSU puts out a course guide which describes courses offered for that quarter and gives a rating according to a student survey. A bad review in the course guide could very well (and often does) result in an empty class for a rather boring professor. The course guide pays for itself by using advertisements from local merchants. It is distributed to the students free of charge.

Columbia Student Agencies

Columbia Student Agencies strives to tap the tremendous New York City market as well as their on-campus clientele. According to Director Eugene Kisluk, the translating service solicits business from local law firms and other companies that need letters, contracts, or documents translated. Columbia students majoring in languages including Chinese, Russian, Japanese, Marathi, Sanskrit, Urdu and Swahili are employed at rates of up to $20 an hour to do this work.

The bartending agency caters to both on and off-campus parties, hiring Columbia students out to serve as bartenders. The tutoring agency is geared more to the on-campus business of helping fellow students cope with their classes.

People with a high entrepreneurial drive tend to get into the business world when they are very young, and seem to be constantly dreaming up new ventures or ways to expand and diversify. You've already met quite a few of these "dynamos," but before I end this section of the book I want to tell you about a few more.

Mr. Video

Brad Pelo started his first videotape business in 1979, when he was a sophomore in high school. According to Brad, one morning he just woke up with the idea of videotaping construction projects and real estate sites. He ripped out all the listings of real estate brokers from the phone book and called them to make appointments. The business did well for a short while, but due to a sluggish real estate market and internal problems of the company, the business closed soon after it opened.

However, Pelo did not give up. Several months later, he got together with three other high school students and started Mountainland Video Productions which makes marketing and training videotapes for corporations. One of the larger contracts they have completed is a training tape for ITT. His firm has also branched out into doing videotapes of parties and weddings. They charge anywhere from $200 to $500 for each tape.

Richmel Inc.

Richard Melcomb started his entrepreneuring long before college. In high school one of his many ventures was the production of a play, Alice in Wonderland, which netted him a few thousand dollars. In his first year at USC he promoted a guitar singer he found "singing in the streets one day." He taped the guitar singer's songs and sent them off to record companies and set up engagements for him at local bars and nightclubs. While he was still an undergraduate economics major at USC he operated three lemonade stands in Los Angeles shopping malls each of them netting him over $300 a day.

After graduation, Melcomb started a new venture, Richmel, Inc., which he currently operates. Richmel markets unique snacks such as "Brownie Points" which Melcomb claims is the "perfect Brownie" and "Demerits" which are neat little licorice candies. With a $10,000 investment made to him by a business associate, Richmel was able to cover the costs of leasing a bakery, packaging and promoting its products. As a result, Richmel succeeded in obtaining orders from major merchandisers such as Macy's, Marshall Fields, and Bloomingdales.

The "Phenomenal" Mike Glickman

Mike Glickman first started building his empire at the age of fifteen when he established the Phenomenal Distribution Company which distributes real estate listings throughout the Los Angeles area. Mike got the idea for his business when he worked for a real estate broker delivering brochures of house listings to other realtors. By the age of nineteen, Glickman had thirty employees delivering real estate listings for his firm. Mike's real estate listing delivery service idea has become very popular across the country. So far, Mike has sold his concept in over sixty-five cities in the United States and Canada. He sells his idea for $1,000 or more, depending on the city. For this fee, he teaches the buyer the business and provides a handbook on how to operate it.

Today at age twenty, Glickman is one of the youngest licensed real estate agents with the San Fernando Valley Board of Realtors and he has sold over $4 million worth of property to this date. In the more exclusive section of Tarzana, where homes list for over $250,000, Glickman is involved in one out of every three real estate transactions.

It is interesting to note that after high school, Glickman spent the summer studying for his real estate exam. After enrolling for college at Cal State Northridge, Glickman passed the examination and went to work for one of the top real estate companies in his area. Glickman saw that the real estate industry offered him an unlimited opportunity and so he decided to devote full time to selling real estate.

Mike has put together a five year plan which he hopes will enable him to establish the largest real estate firm in the San Fernando Valley. He is now two and one-half years into the plan, and in addition to selling $4 million worth of property, he currently has an additional $4 million in inventory. It seems like Glickman's plans are running right on schedule.

Achievement Enterprises, Inc.

"I'm no genius," says Achievement Enterprises' twenty year-old president, Tony Robbins, "but if you want to become successful, you've got to study success, if you want to become happy you've got to study happiness and if you want to become wealthy you've got to study wealth-building. You can't just leave these things to chance, you have got to study them and then you must act upon them!"

Achievement Enterprises' Tony Robbins

Robbins believes that "anyone who has enough desire to learn and act upon their ideas will achieve their goal." Apparently Mr. Robbins has learned his lessons very well. What this young man has done in just a few short years is quite astonishing.

When Robbins was a teenager, his high ambitions sounded crazy to his peers and his family. Tony's parents wanted him just to get through school without taking on too many outside business activities, but Tony didn't want to wait until he finished school to start profiting from his ideas. Some of his ideas seemed pretty far flung to his family and on Christmas Eve, when Tony was sixteen, the household tension caused Tony to leave his home and go off on his own. Tony was able to support himself through high school by holding down a job as a night janitor and doing door-to-door sales. When Robbins was in his senior year at Glendora High School, he was elected president of the student body.

About this time he attended a motivational seminar called "Adventures in Achievement" which was taught by Jim Rohn. Robbins was so impressed with Mr. Rohn's seminar that he decided to work for Mr. Rohn promoting his seminar.

A year later, Robbins decided to start his own seminar brokerage company. Achievement Enterprises, Inc. currently handles the Southern California promotion of numerous reading, nutrition, achievement group dynamics, and real estate seminars. He currently has fifteen full-time employees and he says one of the reasons for his success is that he has managed to surround himself with good, honest people.

Robbins has many other interests. He invests heavily in real estate and also dabbles in the restoration of antique cars. Another of his "hobbies" is finding bright entrepreneurs in different fields and putting together discussion groups he calls "Masterminds" which are designed to dream up new business ideas.

Robbins loves to read. He estimates that in the past three years, he has read over 260 books on goal achievement, wealth building and psychology. He feels that reading is an excellent investment of his time because he can "learn in one hour of reading what it took some other guy ten years to learn."

Kidco, Ltd. Ventures

Probably the most famous young student entrepreneurs in the United States are the four members of the Cessna family who founded Kidco, Ltd. Ventures when they were all between the ages of nine and fourteen. The Cessna kids started out with a street-cleaning operation in their community, sweeping the town's four main streets for a monthly fee of

ids' business venture becomes a clean swe

DONALD COLEMAN
RUNE Business Editor

esident of Kidco, Inc.,
sit behind a big oak desk
and run the affairs of this
used service company.
out with the rest of the
and shovels manure,
e streets of San Diego
states and kills gophers.
he doesn't have a big oak
uses his father's.

Cessna Jr., Kidco's presi-
years old. Other officers
ters Ne-Ne, 9, vice presi-
e, 11, secretary, and June
alf sister), 14, treasurer.
ildren are directors of
company they founded a

year ago in Ramona and which April
1 became incorporated as an
offshore corporation in the Cayman
Islands, a British colony in the West
Indies.

The registration cost $1,500, but
Richard Cessna Sr. said the move
was worth it since Kidco now will not
have to pay income taxes.

"They were moving into the high
tax bracket, because they had no
expenses and most of all their sales
became profits," Cessna said.

Kidco recently turned monthly
revenues of $3,000. Not bad for a
bunch of kids. But, they're not your
everyday bunch. They get everything down in writing — even with
their dad.

Cessna operates the San Diego
Country Estates Equestrian Center
Kidco has a contract with him to
remove wood shavings and horse
manure from the center's 110
stables. The mixture is allowed to
compost, then is sold to local
landscapers and the nearby San Vi-
cente Golf Course.

The children have a deal with San
Diego Country Estates to clean the
main streets of the subdivision for
$150 per month

The contract is to the point. In it
Kidco agrees to: "Pick up trash
Supply vehicle and labor Pick up
once a week. Do a good job."

And in return, the developer "will
pay Kidco $150 per month"

Young Richard said no deal is
made until it's down in writing.
Cessna said he helps the children
in negotiations, "but they make their
own deals. They hammered out a
deal with Bill Watt (subdivision
developer) when they
row mon

brothers and sisters as licensed drivers at $5 per hour. (Cessna and his
wife, Joan, have 10 children).
Cessna said the unde
directore

kill gophers. $1 per h
miss. We fu

State wants back ta from kids' corporo

Kidco, Inc
service comp
dren, may ha
but by no mea

The kids
Board of Equ
ing them fron
the sale of m

"Letters ar
ple concerne
have to pay
reported Pat
service spec
inform the pr
just like any
corporation,
ries are all f
Sund said t
to insure Kic
last year.

It didn't
Richard C
children who
corporation
because whe
corporation
needed the f

"I am hap
will be fill
Cessna lau
ever end fo

SAN DIEGO (AP)—The state Board of Equalization is in-
vestigation an allegation that a horse-manure distribution
firm, whose president is 12, owes back taxes

The action involved KIDCO, Inc., a corporation founded
and run by the children of Richard Cessna, who operates
the equestrian center at San Diego Country Estates, a
planned community in Ramona.

"I think we have a good chance of beating it," said
Richard Cessna Jr., the president of KIDCO "We shouldn't
be taxed" we're just kids. They ought to be glad we're out
working on our own instead of being out someplace, busting
windows".

While the primary service provided by KIDCO is selling
manure and wood shavings from the stable floors in the
form of compost for nurseries and golf courses, KIDCO
also sweeps the streets of the community for $150 per
month, exterminates gophers for $1 each and dabbles in
anything else at which a profit can be turned.

Other officers of the firm, which made $3,000 last Oc-
tober, its best month, are Richard Jr.'s sisters, nine-year-
old NeNe, a vice president; Bette, 11, secretary; and their
half-sister, June Cole, 14, treasurer.

State Draws a Bla
Probe of Gopher Kill

CLARKSTON, WASH.

RAMONA (AP)—The most populous
state in the union conceded today it
can't find out now Dickie Cessna is
killing gophers—for can a make his
tests 12-year-old buy a $50 pesticide
applicator's license.

A pile of

Wed., Apr. 27, 1977

Manurey
Deal

Phila., De

ntroversy Centers on Cessnas

Kids clear air on manure tax

By DONALD COLEMAN
RUNE Business Writer

Kidco, Inc., the Ramona-based service company run by
our children, won its battle with the state Board of
Equalization today and learned that it won't have to pay
back taxes on the sale of manure.

"It appears that Kidco will not have to pay back
taxes," said Richard Morris, Kidco attorney.

Morris made the announcement after he and the four
children and their parents talked with Board of Equalization officials for more than a half-hour behind closed
doors today in the State Office Building.

After the meeting, board officials said the youngsters
will get a seller's permit.

Morris said the ruling is that Kidco does not have to

collect and pay the 6% sales tax on manure used for
agricultural fertilizer.

The tax would have to be paid if the manure were used
to fertilize ornamental plants.

SPOKANE, WASH.. SATURDAY, APRIL 30, 1977.

KIDCO Income
No Child's Play

Kidco Meets Big Brother

Nene Cessna

Bette Cessna   BOARD OF DIRECTORS   Dickie Cessna

June Cole

KIDCO

Kids Sell
The
Manure,
But State
Wants Its
Own Pile

Compromise Fertilizes Young Entrepreneurs' Spirits

Taxes Dull Youngsters'
Sweet Smell Of Success-

Phoenix, Arizona
Phoenix Gazette

Board summons 'dirty' busi

Manure firm checked for tax

Kids Hauled to Court

First gophers, now
Gorda for Kidco

day, April 25, 1977 HONOLULU ADVERTISER

Kid profits
no longer
very stable

idco makes
st political

By BARBARA O'NEIL
T-A Staff Writer

RAMONA — With their profits growing steadily, the four adolescent directors of the service corporation Kidco
Inc. decided that it was time to dabble
in a few little investments.

First they bought some bank stock.
Now they're buying a California town.
Dickie Cessna. 13. Bette Cessna, 12,

Truly, the approximately 20-acre
central California town is a good buy,
especially for those of so few years and
such big plans.

"We probably will put an RV
(recreational vehicle) park there
because it's close to Hearst Castle, you
know," said Dickie, who is Kidco president. "It's a nice town, but we might
change a few things. We might have a

They do say that they want all 21
persons who live there to stay and to
continue to work in the town's store,
restaurant and gas station.

The land deal might astound many,
but, to those who have followed Kidco's
successful history, it's not even surprising The four youthful business tycoons
began a horse manure-selling and
gopher-killing business near their home

12-Yea
Business
Called To

Kidco kids in the news

$100. They later branched out into the fertilizer business by selling manure and wood shavings from the father's stable to the local golf courses, businesses, and residents. They paid their father for the use of his truck, and hired their older brother as a driver. Their fertilizer business became so successful that monthly sales grew to around $3,000. Their next undertaking was a gopher-killing operation.

The Kidco kids have been much in the news not only because of their phenomenal success, but because they ran into problems with a California tax board. (The State wanted to tax their manure sales; the kids claimed the manure was already taxed, on the front end of the horse, in the form of taxes on feed and supplies.)

Another state department soon decided to have its day in court. This time it was the State Department of Food and Agriculture which spent over four months attempting to persuade the kids to reveal the contents of their "secret" homemade gopher killing weapon which they were using to rid their neighbors of gophers for a fee of $1.00 a head. President Dickie Cessna claimed his secret weapon was taught to him by "an old Indian" who lived in the area and that if he let everyone else in on it his business would lose out to his competition. As it turned out, this was one corporate secret that the state was never able to get its hands on.

Kidco's officers soon began to tire of the State's "over-regulation" of their business. After a strategy session, the officers of Kidco decided to appeal to Governor Jerry Brown for help. Dickie, then thirteen, wrote back to the state agriculture people on behalf of his company stating: "We read all the material you sent us about pest control licenses... We even read some of the study books and us little kids don't understand all this stuff. But we do know we are not doing anything that is dangerous to people or birds or other animals. All we do is kill gophers and this is good... We are not trying to be smart alec kids or disrespectful, but we work hard, pay taxes and don't break windows, or steal and the state is always giving us problems making it very tough to stay in business."

The kids' success, government hassles notwithstanding, is nothing short of fantastic. They started in 1976 with an initial investment of $20. In 1980, Kidco's gross income, which included income from movie royalties, TV appearances, commercials, gopher kit sales, T-shirts, and, of course, their original street cleaning, and manure, and gopher-killing businesses, approached three quarters of a million dollars. They have even purchased a small town on the California coast that they plan to turn into a tourist attraction. And all this before their senior member turned seventeen. If they ever decide to go public, I'm buying!

More Money-Making Ideas

William Tobin, a Wilton, Connecticut, editor and publisher, recently gave a speech to a group of local high school students. In his talk, he named thirty money-making ideas that almost anyone could handle, and that require little or no money to start up. I've excerpted a few:

Senior citizen aid services. Use that business title/name. Advertise it with printed bulletins mailed or hand delivered to Wilton homes. Offer TWO services: (1) Companionship—(2) Transportation for the times when it is not available from community social services (late evenings, weekends—odd hours in the morning).

Escort services unlimited. For mothers with youngsters who would like to have a responsible escort take their children to and from school, to the local movie, shopping, or to the town playgrounds, beaches, pools, YWCA. Senior citizens have many needs for escorts: Shopping, walking, companionship, visits to friends, local library, post office, doctor visits, etc. Advertise. Check the Senior Citizens' Center for sales leads. Make up, hand out, a calling card listing your services, name, phone number to every one you meet in local shopping centers.

Qwiktype services. Wilton, *all* of Fairfield County, is the home of hundreds of authors/writers—and businesses—in need of typing assistance, tape transcription, manuscript duplication, and dozens of other quick type services. If you are talented in this area canvass the business centers, call writers/authors listed in the telephone directory, have samples of your work to show.

Research unlimited. Offer your services as a fact-gatherer, researcher. Your local libraries have all the information you need, including a Xerox machine (10¢ a copy) with which to copy needed printed/photographic materials/data/facts. Dozens of local business people need background notes for speeches, market reports, business trends. Local writers and authors regularly employ young people to do factual research.

Tutoring services. IF you are bright (you HAVE TO BE, you're reading this listing!) offer to be of help to parents interested in helping *their* bright or handicapped children do better in their studies. Check the classified ads in local newspapers, parents frequently advertise for help. Have a local printer duplicate 100 sales letters selling your services, mail the letter to 100 homes listed in the telephone directory.

Weekend house watching. Wilton people probably travel, vacation, more frequently than 95% of other Americans. And homes need watching when the owners are away enjoying themselves. You may need a small budget for advertisements in the local papers. A good ad will cost less than $10—and the classified ad people will help you write it—*free.*

House plant/pet care services. This is a yearround, year long, need of hundreds of Wilton homeowners—especially for the times they go out of town on business or visits, or vacation or leave for other reasons. You're in business if you have a bicycle to make your rounds.

NOTE: Businesses are never static, and student-run businesses tend to be in a greater state of flux than any other. Students graduate, transfer, and drop out, and when they do, they close up their businesses, sell them, or expand them to make full time careers of them. So, while I have tried to be as up-to-date as possible with this material, many of the businesses discussed in this book will not be operating today exactly as they are described.

SECTION THREE

General Planning

Once you've decided on an idea for your new business venture, you must develop a very well-defined and detailed plan to carry it out. At this stage, you need to make a thorough study of your business idea and of the market you're going to sell to, and you must think about *how* you will sell your product. As a student, time will probably be of major concern to you—so before you start, analyze how you can design your business to fit in with your school or work schedule. You should also plan a budget of operating expenses. Finally, you can do some background work on business management. (Those of you in business school or in an entrepreneurial course should be one step ahead on this one.)

This planning stage is critical, because it will help you avoid pitfalls and keep you out of trouble, and will help you tailor your operation to fit your resources and needs. So avert disaster—look before you leap! As a matter of fact, this research may tell you not to leap at all, that your idea is not going to work. In that case, you'll be back at square one and will have to dream up a new scheme. But don't worry—you've only lost a little time, whereas if you'd plunged into an ill-fated business venture, you'd probably lose a lot of time, and whatever money you've invested, too.

Researching the Business

Remember the first commandment in sales: Thou shalt know thy product! If you don't truly understand the product or service you are selling, you are bound for trouble. So read up on it (through trade journals, catalogues, manufacturers' ads, etc.), talk to suppliers, to professionals in your field, or to others running similar businesses. Don't be afraid to ask questions—you may unearth some vital information. Besides, the more you know about your competition, the better off you will be.

If you know your product's selling points, strengths, guarantees, accessories, uses, etc., you'll be in a good position to increase your sales. If you know your product's weak points and maintenance requirements, you'll be prepared to deal with problems that may arise.

As you do this research, keep records of sources, prices, shipping details, payment schedules—anything that might prove useful to you later on. If your business is going to require you to rent space for storage or for the operation of the business itself, you will need to start shopping around for that at this time, too. There's no need to sign any papers yet, but you should begin looking into availability, location and rental fees of suitable spaces.

Researching the Market

Although you may be absolutely in love with your business idea, you may find out that nobody else shares your feelings, in which case you are going to get burned. The trick in proper business planning is to try to prevent any such unpleasant surprises. So try to find out in advance if there really is a market for your product. To put it plainly, will anyone buy?

The best way to find out is to run a quick survey. If it's cookies you are interested in selling, try knocking on a few doors at different dorms and ask your fellow students if they would buy big chocolate chip cookies at thirty-five cents each if you would sell them door-to-door in the evening. While you're at it, you might as well ask them when is the best time to catch them, and when they get most hungry.

Even the sharpest people will forget this very basic step. Don't be one of them. Do a little inquiring, make a few phone calls, run a pilot ad, send out a few letters. Don't be afraid to take the initiative.

This basic market research should help you zero in on just who you need to reach with your advertising campaigns, and give you a clearer idea of where you are going to sell your product (are you going to your customers, or will they come to you?) and when you will conduct your business. Obviously, you want to sell at a time when your customers are most accessible, but at the same time you have to fit your own time obligations into that framework. I will go into the matter of scheduling more thoroughly in the following section.

Analyzing Time and Money

Based on the information you've so far gathered, you can begin to outline your business plan more fully, hoping to integrate it with your time availability and your financial resources.

The first thing to do is to get a general idea of what your starting-up expenses are going to be. This, of course, will depend on the type of business you're setting up. You can start your own roommate-finding service with little more than a few ads in the college paper, an answering service, and some file cards, whereas putting on sound and light shows for parties will require some expensive equipment plus a van or truck for transporting it. Be as complete as you can in drawing up a list of basic supplies and inventory, equipment, etc. Don't forget to include money for licenses and permits if you are required to have them (we will discuss this later), the cost of an answering service or rental or storage space if you need them, and initial advertising.

Now take a look at your bank book and see if you're going to be able to finance your new venture. If it looks tight, there are several things you can do. You can borrow money from family or friends. You can hang onto the part-time job you have (if you have one) until the business starts bringing in some money. Or you could find a partner who will share the costs of going into business. Keep in mind that your business will most likely require additional expenses other than the initial investment to keep it going in the beginning stages. Costs add up 50 percent faster than your most liberal estimates, and under-capitalization and cash-flow problems are two of the main reasons businesses fail. The first few weeks may be tough, and you may not see as much cash coming in as going out. But if you hang in there long enough, you will start establishing yourself and turning a profit.

So start small with the least possible investment, and keep initial expenses to a minimum. Once your business starts making a profit, you can then expand.

Your next big consideration is the time factor. When I first started out on my own business, I used to think that time was my second most valuable resource (money being the first). I've come to believe they are equally valuable, and that you should spend time like you spend money. Plan it, manage it, and keep a record of it.

I have found the time chart from the Learning Assistance Center at Stanford an invaluable aid to managing my time. Using this chart, I block out all the chunks of time that are regularly committed—classes, meetings, activities. Then I know exactly what time I have left for study, and for tending to the business. I keep one copy of my chart posted on my wall, and another in my wallet so I always know what my free times are. You can use a similar system to plot out your available time against the time your business will require to see if you are going to have any major conflicts. (See Figure 1.)

I also suggest that you carry a small pocket calendar with you so you

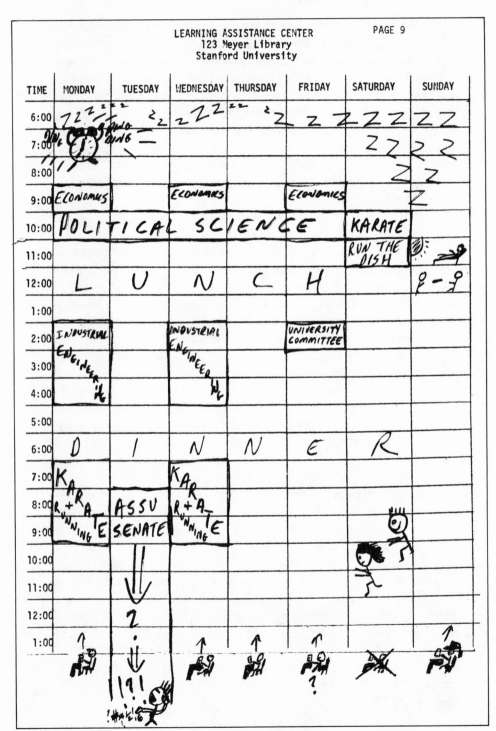

Figure 1 – Time Chart

can write down all your appointments as soon as you make them. This will not only help you manage your time more efficiently, but it will prevent you from forgetting appointments and running into conflicts. You should also get in the habit of writing down ideas as they occur to you, and reminders of things that need doing. It's much easier to organize your time, chores, —your life—if you just get it down on paper. Try it for a week, and you'll see that the improvement is well worth the effort.

Partnerships

The average student is going to be severely pressed for time and money. For this reason, many enterprises get started as partnerships, something you may want to consider after analyzing your own resources. A partner can share the workload, add ideas, provide companionship, and help finance the concern.

Finding a good partner is not a simple matter, however, and bears careful consideration. Friends may or may not be the answer, because there is much more than friendship involved. There is shared responsibility and there are business qualifications to be considered. You also have to be sure you'll be able to work well with your partner, and that this person is properly motivated to handle running a business.

The ideal partnership is built on a perfect blend of complementary strengths. One partner may have the salesmanship, the other a head for figures. One may be the inventor, the other the planner who executes the scheme. In a good business "marriage" each partner will bring out the best in the other. Venture capitalists, as a matter of fact, strongly favor financing a new business backed by a management team over one run by a lone entrepreneur. Management teams show better success records because the partners can rely on each other to share experience, personal resources, and workload.

Kingstone Bedding Warehouse

Now I'd like to show you how I fit all these pieces together to start my own business, the Kingstone Bedding Warehouse, which sold electric adjustable beds. I chose this particular business for several reasons. First of all, I was familiar with the bedding industry since my family owned a mattress factory and I had worked there. I knew that Niagara, the nation's leading competitor in this market, was enjoying good sales of its product. I was aware of the tremendous amount of television advertising by national adjustable bed firms and felt I could take advantage of this good publicity.

I studied bedding trade journals (and consulted with my father) and located a Los Angeles manufacturer of adjustable beds. This company was well known in the industry for high quality and good product guarantees. The fact that their factory is located on the west coast and that they do not engage in costly national advertising has enabled them to offer better quality adjustable beds at prices ranging from one hundred fifty to three hundred dollars below the national brand's suggested retail price. Due to my company's low overhead costs, I was able to bring the price down on each bed an additional one hundred and fifty dollars on the average. After weighing all these considerations, I decided to take the risk of making the initial investment to start my business. I contacted the manufacturer and they agreed to grant me a distributorship in the San Francisco Bay Area.

One of my main concerns when I was deciding to start my business was how much investment in terms of time and money my business would require. Since I was a full time student at Stanford, I did not want to undertake any project that would require so much time that it might jeopardize my college career. Likewise, I had a limited amount of "expendable" finances above what I needed for tuition and expenses that I was willing to commit to a new business venture. I did not want to "get in over my head."

So, after making the tentative decision to go into the electric bed business, it was essential to figure out if I could manage the time to run the business, and if I could handle it financially. I blocked out my time commitments on the Learning Assistance Center's chart and decided that if I did not run for re-election for the Student Senate I would gain eleven hours a week. I felt this would work out because the beds are a high priced item that would sell at a high profit per sale and require little "in-store" time. (The lower priced your product, the more sales you must make to cover overhead, and the more time it will take.) In addition, I planned to arrange appointments to make the sales in my spare time, and there would be little time wasted.

The next consideration was money. I needed two display models, which would be a major investment. Since I was selling an expensive product which required a maintenance guarantee and hence consumer trust, I had to have all the necessary business licenses to present to my customers. I also needed to pay for advertising and for an answering service. I figured this would all add up to about $850, which I could finance with savings.

Before investing in two costly display models, I did some preliminary market testing. (Remember, find out if anybody's going to buy before you go into business!) I placed small advertisements in retirement communities and apartment houses. I showed my prospective customers brochures and described the good quality of the beds and pointed out the 30 to 50 percent savings I would be offering off the price of nationally advertised brands. The response to my ads was good, but most people wanted to test the product before buying. After weighing all the information I'd gathered, I decided to take the risk, invest in the display models, and fully start up the business.

Having made this decision, the next step was to arrange for a place to conduct the business, and for receiving, storing and delivering the beds. Fortunately, I was able to resolve all these problems fairly simply. The previous summer, I had stored my motorcycle at a moving and storage warehouse in San Carlos. The warehouse was in excellent condition and is in a good location (right off Highway 101). The owner, Mr. Jim Taylor, was a very friendly man and we developed a good rapport with each other. I decided to approach him with my business idea to see if he would allow me to store my merchandise at his warehouse and set up a small display. Mr. Taylor was in the moving business and he had trucks that were able to handle the deliveries of my merchandise. We were able to come to an agreement whereby Mr. Taylor would handle the deliveries of all my merchandise for a charge of 10 percent of the overall purchase price of each bed. In addition, he granted me warehousing and display space for my beds.

This warehouse agreement was ideal because it enabled me to have one company that would handle all the receivables, storage, display, and deliveries for my company. In addition, my expenses and cash flow were controlled because I did not have a running weekly overhead. Instead, I only paid a percentage of what I sold and thus I was able to pay when I made money. This greatly limited the initial amount of investment I had to risk.

I later capitalized on the idea of using a warehouse to operate my business by naming my company Kingstone Bedding Warehouse and advertising the great savings my company offered by selling these adjustable beds direct from the warehouse to the consumer. In all my newspaper and direct mail ads, I stated that the warehouse was only open to the public on Saturdays from 10 am to 6 pm. The ads also stated that customers can call our answering service to receive more information. Thus, I was able to limit my "in store" time to just one day a week. I was able to handle all inquiries and calls in my spare time after checking with my answering service.

After operating my business for three weeks, and talking with my customers, I learned that setting up appointments at a customer's home might be a better way to market my product. So when I received calls from prospective customers, I would set up an appointment at their home, usually on a Saturday when I had a few other appointments set up. I would then rent a van and transport the display model to their homes and give the sales pitch. When my percentage of sales proved to be much higher using this method, I completely switched to this sales method. I also found out that, in the long run, it saved me a lot of time because I didn't have to wait around for customers in my warehouse all day.

Small Business Management

Take time during the planning stage to learn as much as you can about how to run a small business, using all the resources available to you. One of the best sources of information is the U.S. Small Business Administration. To find the SBA office closest to you, call the Federal Information number listed under U.S. Government in your local phone directory. (For a full national listing of SBA offices write to: Office of Advocacy, Small Business Administration, 1441 L Street, Washington, D.C. 20416, and ask for their *Directory of State Small Business Services*.) Then find out what your local SBA office has to offer. You may be able to join a one-day seminar, or make an appointment for a consultation. The SBA has a comprehensive series of free publications. Take advantage of this service, too, and ask for any that you think might be useful to you. (See Appendix A.)

In many areas, there are groups of retired businessmen who volunteer to help people get started in business. In San Jose, I received help from just such a group. (It is called SCORE, the Service Corps of Retired Executives. I contacted them through the San Jose Chamber of Commerce.) In New York City, there is the Executive Volunteer Corps. When I was in New York doing research for this book, I utilized their service, and I'd like to thank my counselor, Mr. Seymour Miller, for a job well done. (See Figures 2 and 3.)

I also attended a very informative one-day seminar on small business management. The seminar was taught by Bernard Kamoroff, CPA, and was sponsored by Open Education Exchange.

Many banks provide free small business management guides which are extremely helpful, so check your local banks. You can also get advice from your faculty sponsor, if you have one, or from counselors or professors at your school. And don't forget, your fellow student entrepreneurs may be the best source of information of all.

SCORE

SCORE CAN HELP YOU!

SCORE, the Service Corps of Retired Executives, is a volunteer group of retired men and women who provide free management counseling to small business owner/managers and those who are considering starting a business. Sponsored by the U.S. Small Business Administration, SCORE was developed by SBA in 1964 as a means of tapping the vast business expertise of the growing ranks of top-notch retired executives for the benefit of America's business community.

Use of good business management skills is the most important factor in running a successful small business. SCORE Counselors know that no two businesses are alike, so they are prepared to listen to your plans or problems and discuss them with you. They never attempt to run your business. Their advice is always forthright and honest, because they have no axe to grind and no profits to make from any counseling contacts. SCORE volunteers counsel both at the SCORE Chapter offices and at the small business locations to which they are assigned.

HOW CAN I GET SCORE HELP?

Call the San Jose Chamber of Commerce, (408) 998-7000 or call the nearest office of the U.S. Small Business Administration listed in your telephone directory under "U.S. Government."

Or complete the attached form and mail it to: SCORE, San Jose Chamber of Commerce, One Paseo De San Antonio, San Jose, CA 95113.

07-300-12/79

One Paseo de San Antonio, San Jose, California 95113, Telephone: (408) 998-7000

Figure 2 – Score Fact Sheet

Do you have a business problem?
Are you starting a new business?

**You can benefit from FREE, expert, confidential
advice from successful business executives.**

Telephone: (212) 697-2101

COME TO NUMBER ONE
THE EXECUTIVE VOLUNTEER CORPS
SIDNEY KUSHIN, COMMISSIONER
41 EAST 42nd STREET, NEW YORK, N.Y. 10017

The City of New York / Edward I. Koch, Mayor / Peter J. Solomon, Deputy Mayor For Economic Policy & Development

What Is The Executive Volunteer Corps?

The Executive Volunteer Corps is staffed by successful, retired businessmen who have had
wide management experience. These counselors, each a former leader in his field, offer free,
expert business advice.

**How Can The Executive Volunteer Corps Help
You Solve Your Business Problem?**

When you visit the Executive Volunteer Corps, your problem is examined by a counselor who
is likely to have solved a similar difficulty when operating his own business. Because each
counselor specializes in a particular kind of business, the Executive Volunteer Corps can offer
a broad range of advice and assistance.

Will The Counselor Visit Your Place Of Business To Help You?

Yes. If, following a conference with you at our office, your counselor believes he can best help
you by visiting your place of business, he will do so.

**Why Does The City Government Care
About Your Business Problems?**

The success of your business is vital to New York City. Thriving businesses produce employment opportunities for our citizens and tax revenues for the municipal treasury. However,
business failures leave unemployment, empty stores and empty factories in their wake. If New
York is to enjoy a healthy commercial climate, new businesses must be properly operated in
order to have every chance of prospering.

100M-X201230(80)

Figure 3 – Executive Volunteer Corps Flyer

Before you start, you should ask yourself some questions about your business idea, your market, and your sales plan. These questions may seem very obvious, even silly, to you, but the answers to them are a very serious part of planning. Besides, it is too easy to overlook the obvious. So ask yourself these questions, jot down a few notes after each one, and use them to formulate your final business plan.

Ten Questions You Should Ask:

1. Why Am I Starting My Own Business?

2. What Type of Business Do I Want?

3. Do I Have Enough Time and Money?

4. What Am I Selling?

5. Who Am I Selling To?

6. Will They Buy?

7. Where Will I Sell It?

8. When Will I Sell It?

9. How Will I Sell It?

10. Should I Do It?

Weighing Advantages and Disadvantages

All of the points I've covered so far in this section were designed to help you answer that one last question—*Should I Do It?* or, to put it another way, *Can I Make a Go of It?* To answer this question, you'll need to weigh all the information you've gathered so far about the nature of your business and the time and money factors involved. Before you make your final decision there are a couple of additional factors you should consider, too, and here we come to a more sobering part of this book.

I guess I could have dubbed my book "How to Make Mega-Bucks" or "How I Paid My Education Expenses by Simply Investing Ten Hours a Week," but although these titles would have strongly described the possible benefits of being an entrepreneur, they would not have presented a full picture of the situation. Because there *are* disadvantages to being an entrepreneur, and you should be aware of them before you embark on a new enterprise.

First and foremost, you must understand that going into business always entails a risk. There are no guarantees of success; you may never realize one cent of profit. In fact, the IRS reports that 50 percent of all businesses fail in the first year, and of those remaining, 50 percent more fail in the second year.

Then you must consider that your income may not be a steady one. New businesses often go through a rough starting-up period, and even established businesses have their good weeks and bad weeks. So you must realize that your income will probably go up and down, especially in the beginning. One way to get around this is to hang on to your regular part-time job until you have a fairly steady *average* income with your new business.

Not only will your income go up and down, the demands on your time will, too. In the initial stages, expect to put in more time. If you are hanging on to a part-time job, too, you may begin to feel strapped for time, but this situation should just be temporary. It may mean cutting down on extracurricular activities for a while, but you can resume them once you settle into a comfortable working schedule.

On the other hand, there are plenty of advantages to running your own business. I'll tell you what it meant to me: *Money, Experience, Academic Credit,* and *Excitement!*

Running your own business means creating an opportunity for almost unlimited *income*. Running the Kingstone Bedding Warehouse, I made well over three times the salary per hour that I would have at any typical part-time student job. (If you consider the tax benefits of running your own business, which I will discuss later, that rate would be even higher.) In fact, while I was operating it, during my junior year, my business was paying for much of my educational expenses.

The *experience* you will gain by running your own business will be invaluable. Classroom study or part-time student jobs just cannot compare with "hands on" practical experience. Managing your own business is definitely a refreshing alternative to highly theoretical, often impractical, economics courses that are far too common in undergraduate programs. And when you graduate into the "real" world of business, that experience is bound to stand you in good stead.

It is quite possible you will be able to obtain *academic credit* through a university department for running your "business project." As I said earlier, I was granted five units of credit in one semester for reporting on the management and operation of my business, and I recommend that all student entrepreneurs ask for similar credit (see page 147).

Running your own business can be fun and *exciting*. It is a great feeling to be your own boss, to wake up in the morning and decide how many hours you want to put in, and to set your own profit goals each week rather than to plod away at some part-time job every day. When you're your own boss, you'll be in full control of your own work, and will be able to utilize your imagination and abilities to their highest potentials. When profits start to grow, you'll have the satisfaction of knowing that you were directly responsible for your own success.

Are You an Entrepreneur?

Now for the final consideration, and that is whether or not you are the type of person who can make it as an entrepreneur. Every successful entrepreneur that I've interviewed has been ambitious, enthusiastic, creative, energetic, and a little bit daring. If you don't have these qualities in some measure, your chances of success are not great—if the thought of being your own boss, and of being responsible for making decisions, scares you maybe you'd better throw this book away. Unfortunately, while this book can give you some good ideas and tell you how to plan and organize, it cannot teach you ambition or enthusiasm.

Student Entrepreneur Quiz

1. Are you ambitious?

2. Do you enjoy a good challenge?

3. Do you set high goals for yourself?

4. Are you competitive and success oriented?

5. Are you willing to take risks to make a profit?

6. Are you creative?

7. Do you get enthusiastic about your ideas?

8. Would you rather lead than follow?

9. Do you feel confident in your ability to work on your own?

10. Do you expect more out of life than just a good salary and a steady job?

If you answered yes to all these questions, then you are just the type of person who can succeed as an entrepreneur!

Entrepreneurial Personality Quiz

Are you tough enough to be an entrepreneur? Do you have what it takes to start up your own business? We've put together a list of questions, based on Alan Jacobowitz's theory of entrepreneurial personality, that you can try to measure up against.

1. Were your parents, close relatives, or close friends entrepreneurs?

2. Did any of that business carry over into your home when you were growing up?

3. Did you have a lemonade stand or a paper route as a kid?

4. Was your academic record in school less than outstanding?

5. Did you feel like an outsider among peers at school?

6. Were you often reprimanded for your school behavior?

7. Do you have difficulty attaining satisfaction from any job with a large firm?

8. Do you often feel that you could do a better job than your boss?

9. Would you rather play sports than watch them on television?

10. Do you prefer nonfiction to fiction?

11. Have you ever been fired from a job or left one under pressure?

12. Do you never lose sleep at night over your work or personal business?

13. Would you rather jump into a project than plan one?

14. Would you consider yourself decisive, a good thinker on your feet?

15. Are you active in community affairs?

If you answered yes to 12 or more of these questions and you are not an entrepreneur already, you may be missing your big chance. If you answered yes to fewer than 12 and you already are an entrepreneur...well, good luck!

Getting Started

The Business Plan:
Getting it All Down on Paper

When you first think about starting your own business hundreds of thoughts, ideas, and questions will race through your mind. I have one important suggestion: *Write Them Down!* Not only will it keep you from forgetting, it will help you to develop a clearer picture of what your business is, what it needs, and where it is heading. From this collection of thoughts and ideas, you should write some sort of organized business plan for your new venture which you will use as a road map to guide you to success. I have learned from experience, and from talking with other entrepreneurs, that the best laid plans are those that are put in writing.

There are many texts and handbooks which describe how to write business plans. Some go into greater detail than a part-time student business will need—a five-year financial statement or projection would rarely be called for. What should suffice is a general outline of your idea, start up costs, operating expenses, and sales strategy. Here is a brief general outline which you can use to develop your own business plan:

1. The Idea: Describe your business product or service idea.

2. Your Goals: Describe the objectives of your company.

3. The Market: Describe your market. Who are your potential customers?

4. Your Competition: Compare your product or service to similar ones already on the market. Who is your competition?

5. Sales Strategy: How will you sell your product or service? What will be your company's advertising policy?

6. Product Cost and Price: How much does your product cost? How much will you charge and what will be the method of payment? Be sure your income will cover your expenses. Remember, cash flow and liquidity are important.

7. *Sales Quotas:* How many items will you need to sell (or how many jobs will you need to complete) in order to make a profit? Based on your market research, what is a reasonable quota?

8. *Service or Warranties:* How will you deal with repairs or defective merchandise?

9. *Operations Plan:* Plan location of sales, and location of office. Where will you obtain materials and supplies? Where will you store them?

10. *Partners and/or Employees:* Do you want either? If so, write out a job description and a list of responsibilities for each partner or employee, including yourself. Define what the jobs will be ahead of time!

11. *Time Schedule:* Set target dates for obtaining licenses, manufacturing your first products, opening your sales doors, meeting your first quotas, etc. Make an advanced calendar for your business which you can work by.

12. *Financing:* Where will your money come from—personal savings, friendly investors, relatives, banks, venture capitalists, or sale of stock? (Note: If you need to borrow money, a well thought out business plan will probably be the key ingredient in convincing an investor to back your business.) Make sure that all your loans and investment agreements are put in writing and signed. *Make sure* that you *fully understand* these agreements!

13. *The Financial Plan:* Make a budget list of your start up costs (licenses, materials, supplies, tools, painting, answering service, etc.) Make an estimated first year balance sheet and income statement. For sophisticated businesses, most textbooks call for three to five-year projections. Part-time student entrepreneurs don't need this. You should, however, consult an accounting text to acquaint yourself with a balance sheet and income statement and make a rough estimate of your profit expectations based on anticipated expenses and income. Multiply your sales quota by the prices you expect to charge to determine your income for a set period of time.

The "bottom line" of your business plan is your profit estimate. This will be looked at very carefully by potential investors. You should look at it very closely, too. It could show you ahead of time if you have planned well and if this business venture is really going to be worth your efforts. Even if your business is a very simple one involving only a few hours a week, you should make some sort of profit estimate. If you're going to make little or no money, then perhaps you'd better rework your product costs plan, pricing strategy, sales quota, or possibly the entire business idea.

Licenses and Permits

If your business is a very simple one, you may be able to get by without a business license or seller's permit—a cookie service that deals with fellow students and has low revenues, for instance, might skip the formalities—but any company that deals with "the outside world" will find it both a legal and social necessity to possess the required state, county, and local permits. In the long run, though, no matter what type of part-time business you intend to operate, I think you will find it beneficial to spend the extra $10 to $50 to become a legal business just for the experience of doing so.

This section describes the licenses I needed for my business. They are typical of licensing requirements everywhere. However, because each city, county, and state may have slightly different regulations, you will need to check with the appropriate government offices to get the most current information on legal requirements in your own particular location, and for your particular business. You should also be aware that government, on all levels, has an infamous passion for making new regulations and revising old ones. So use this section as a general guideline only, and, as I said before, always get the latest information from the proper authorities. Your local SBA office can assist you here.

State Seller's Permit

In states which have a sales tax, all sellers of goods designated for resale direct to the consumer ("retail sales") must collect sales taxes. In these states you must have a State Seller's Permit or Resale Permit. This is an official permit to sell, and automatically registers you as a collector of state sales taxes. It also enables you to buy goods for resale from a wholesaler without having to pay a sales tax yourself. As a retailer, you will be responsible for keeping track of taxes collected. You will receive a form (usually quarterly) from the state which you fill out and send back with the taxes you've collected. If your business is strictly a service business (homesitting, maintenance) you won't need the permit. If you are operating a manufacturing or "middle man" wholesale company and deal only with retailers, not consumers, again, you will not need the resale permits.

I obtained two permits (Figure 4)—one which listed my warehouse address, and another which listed my dorm address. (They were in different counties, and I wanted to be licensed to sell in both counties.) It was a simple matter to fill out the application forms (Figure 5), and they were processed on the spot, free of charge. In California, the State Board of Equalization issues these permits. In other states, the office may be known as the State Department of Revenue or the State Sales and Income Tax Office.

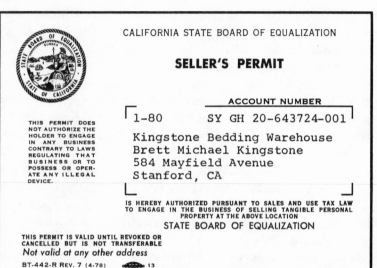

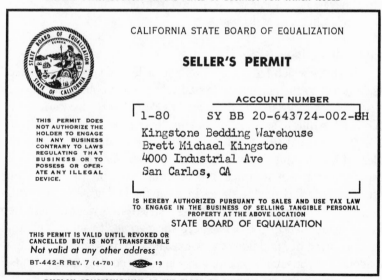

Figure 4 – Seller's Permit

BT-400 REV. 23 (5-79)

**APPLICATION FOR SELLER'S PERMIT AND
REGISTRATION AS A RETAILER
AND
EMPLOYMENT DEVELOPMENT DEPARTMENT
REGISTRATION AS AN EMPLOYER**

STATE OF CALIFORNIA
BOARD OF EQUALIZATION
DEPARTMENT OF BUSINESS TAXES

1. Office	55	03	1/17/80 Date	2. HQ Registration Unit		Date

3. Reinstatement Fee		4. Are You Buying a Business?	5. Date of Purchase	7. Account Number		
Amount	Receipt Number	Yes ☐ All ☐ Part ☐		Tax	Office	Number
$		No ☒ Reorganization ☐	6. Purchase Price	SR	GH	

8. Owner(s)

BRETT MICHAEL KINGSTONE

9. Firm Name 2201   KINGSTONE BEDDING WAREHOUSE   /N.

10. Location of Business: 584 Mayfield Avenue	Street & Number	Stanford City or Town 11	/	State CA	Zip Code 94305	24

11. Mailing Address (if different from above): 10 P.O. Box or Street & Number		City or Town 11	/	State CA	Zip Code	12

12. Type of Organization: Husband and Wife Co-ownership ☐
Individual ☒ Partnership ☐ Corporation ☐ Other ☐

13. Corporation Officers: President   Vice-President   Secretary   Treasurer

14. Name of Former Owner	Business Name of Former Owner	Former Owner's Account Number

15. Type or Nature of Business (If Mixed, Underscore Principal Types and Product)
mattresses and bedding

Check *Principal Activity:*
Retailing ☒ Manufacturing ☐ Jobbing, or Wholesaling ☐ Repairing ☐   Performing Business, Professional or Personal Services ☐   Construction Contractor ☐   Type of A.B.C. License

16. Part Time?	Itinerant	Is Business Located Within City Limits?	18. **REGISTRATION — EMPLOYMENT DEVELOPMENT DEPARTMENT**
No ☐ Yes ☒	No ☒ Yes ☐	No ☐ Yes ☒	A. Are you now registered as an Employer under the California Unemployment Insurance Code? No ☒ Yes ☐
Date Started This Address	1/21/80		B. Do you have more than one establishment? No ☒ Yes ☐

17. FOR DISTRICT USE ONLY
Any Delinquencies for Prior Periods? No ☒ Yes ☐
If Yes for What Period? _____
Action Taken to Clear _____
New ☒ Temporary ☐ Issue & Cancel (Attach BT-406) ☐

NO
EDD { Reinstatement After Revocation ☐
COPY { Reinstatement After Revocation & After Close-out ☐
Reinstate. After Revocation & Interdistrict Move (Att. BT-1047) ☐

C. Account Number _____
D. Business Name _____
E. Will your payroll exceed $100 in any calendar quarter? No 0 Yes ☐
F. Quarter ending date Mo.___Year___Number of Employees_____
G. Enter first month that worker contributions for disability insurance exceeds $50 OR personal income tax withheld exceeds $100_____
H. Did you acquire all or only part of the seller's business? All ☐ Part ☐
I. Federal Employer Identification Number _____

STAPLE NUMERIC FILE CARD HERE

19.

Basis	Bus. Code	Area Code Co.	Jur.	Original Starting Date Month	Year	Owner Code	Account Analysis	FOR HEADQUARTERS USE ONLY					O.S. Audit Office	Transit District Code	Except. Code	Special Return Processing Code	Ext. Code
								Effective Date			O.S. Location						
								Month	Day	Year	State	Zip					
Q	29	43	06	01	80	S			01								

20. Furnished to Taxpayer:
Notice of Prepayment Status Form BT-1241 ☐
Form BT-741 ☐
Regulation 1700 ☒
Regulations _____

21. *FILING INSTRUCTIONS:*
You are *quarterly* notified that you are required to file sales and use tax returns and pay tax on a calendar basis. Returns are due on or before the last day of the first month following the close of the reporting period.

22. CERTIFICATE: THE ABOVE STATEMENTS ARE HEREBY CERTIFIED TO BE CORRECT TO THE BEST KNOWLEDGE AND BELIEF OF THE UNDERSIGNED WHO IS DULY AUTHORIZED TO SIGN THIS APPLICATION.

Signature X *Brett Kingstone*   Title Owner   Date 1/17/80
Residence Address line 10
Residence Phone 327-8988   Business Phone 321-8780
Driver's License Number H9261980
Social Security Number 099-54-3469

Returns No ☒ Yes ☐
Periods _____

23. TRANSIT DISTRICT INFORMATION
You are further notified that if your location of business is in a transit district which imposes a transactions (sales) tax and use tax, or if you engage in business in such a district (see Section 9 on the reverse of this application and Form BT-741, Your Privileges and Obligations As A Seller, attached), you are required to report the applicable transit district tax on your State, Local and District Sales and Use Tax Return.

APPLICANT'S COPY

77918-C 550 5-79 180M QUAD OSP

Figure 5 – Application for Seller's Permit

State Employer's Registration Form

Most states will only require you to register as an employer if you are going to hire someone besides yourself. California has a single form which combines the application for a seller's permit and the registration as an employer. Since I did not plan to hire an employee, I simply indicated so on the registration form. If you plan to hire help, you will need to register as an employer with your state employment department. (You will also need to register with the federal government. More on this later.)

"Doing Business As" or Fictitious Business Name Statement

The "Doing Business As" (DBA) statement registers the name of your business and its function, and registers you as its owner. You will need an official copy of your DBA in order to establish a business bank account. In California, the DBA statement must be filed in the county where the business has its home office; that is, where the business keeps its books. This allows the county to keep a record of the company and its owner. (See Figure 6.)

My county charged a $10 filing fee for this statement, and also required that the statement be published four times at one week intervals, in a local newspaper. This serves as a legal pronouncement that you intend to establish a business in the county. It cost $28 for the newspaper announcement. (See Figure 7.)

Incidentally, new business entrepreneurs will soon find out that these published statements also attract many business services which will be contacting you by phone or mail. Within one week of publication of my DBA, I was contacted by a business printing shop and two business credit and finance institutions.

Local Business Requirements

After filing for and obtaining the necessary state and county licenses my last step was to find out and fulfill the requirements of the cities in which I planned to operate my business. My home office, located at Stanford, was under the jurisdiction of the city of Palo Alto. I called the Palo Alto city clerk's office and was informed that the city does not require any business licenses. As for my warehouse, which was located in San Carlos, I was informed by their City Clerk that I needed a zoning permit to approve the warehousing of my merchandise at that location and a city business license. So off I went to the San Carlos City Hall to file for a zoning permit and a business license. The zoning permit cost $10 and took five minutes to fill out. The business license normally costs $50 but their licensing year starts in June, so since I filed in January, I had to pay only $25 for a half

A MAIL CERTIFIED COPIES TO:	B PUBLISH IN
NAME Brett Kingstone	COUNTY CLERK'S FILING STAMP
ADDRESS 584 Mayfield Ave.	**FILED**
CITY Stanford, CA. 94305	JAN 18 1980
	JOHN KAZUBOWSKI, Clerk
	E. A. FLORES Deputy

FICTITIOUS BUSINESS NAME STATEMENT
THE FOLLOWING PERSON(S) IS (ARE) DOING BUSINESS AS:

1.* Fictitious Business Name(s)

Kingstone Bedding Warehouse

2.** Street Address, City & State of Principal place of Business in California   Zip Code

584 Mayfield Ave. Stanford, CA 94305

3.***

Full Name of Registrant	Full Name of Registrant
Brett Michael Kingstone	
(if corporation, show state of incorporation)	(if corporation, show state of incorporation)
584 Mayfield Ave.	
Residence Address	Residence Address
Stanford, California 94305	
City State Zip	City State Zip
Full Name of Registrant	Full Name of Registrant
(if corporation, show state of incorporation)	(if corporation, show state of incorporation)
Residence Address	Residence Address
City State Zip	City State Zip

4.**** This business is conducted by (X) an individual ( ) individuals (Husband & Wife) ( ) a general partnership ( ) a limited partnership ( ) an unincorporated association other than a partnership ( ) a corporation ( ) a business trust (CHECK ONE ONLY)

5.A

Signed _Brett Kingstone_

Typed or Printed   Brett Kingstone

5.B   If Registrant a corporation sign below:

Corporation Name _____

Signature & Title _____

Type or Print
Officer's Name & Title _____

This statement was filed with the County Clerk of   Santa Clara   County on date indicated by file stamp above.

6. New Fictitious Business Name Statement	I HEREBY CERTIFY THAT THIS COPY IS A CORRECT COPY OF THE ORIGINAL STATEMENT ON FILE IN MY OFFICE.
	JOHN KAZUBOWSKI
	COUNTY CLERK
7. Refile — Statement expires December 31.	BY _____ DEPUTY
File No. _____	File No. _____ 53279

This form is provided free of charge by the following "Newspapers of General Circulation"

Figure 6 – Fictitious Business Name Statement

Proof of Publication

(2015.5 C.C.P.)

ADVOCATE JOURNAL
15 N. MARKET ST. \ SAN JOSE, CA 95113
(408) 292-7833

Space Below for Use of County Clerk Only

(ENDORSED)
FILED
FEB 26 1980

JOHN KAZUBOWSKI, Clerk
Deputy

SUPERIOR COURT OF THE STATE OF CALIFORNIA
FOR THE COUNTY OF SANTA CLARA

No. 53279 ....

...... FICTITIOUS. BUSINESS. NAME ...
STATEMENT
....
....
....
....

State of California
County of Santa Clara,ss

I, the undersigned,state that I am, and at all times herein mentioned, was a citizen of the United States of America, over the age of eighteen years and not a party to or interested in the above entitled matter; that I am the principal clerk of the publisher of the Advocate Journal, a newspaper of general circulation, published Tuesdays and Fridays in the City of San Jose, County of Santa Clara, which newspaper has been adjudged a neswpaper of general circulation by Superior Court of the County of Santa Clara, State of California, on October 1, 1976, Case Number 359645, and that the notice of which the annexed is a printed copy, has been published in each regular and entire issue of said newspaper and not in any supplement thereof, on the following dates to wit: Feb. 5, 12, 19, 26

I declare under penalty of perjury that the foregoing is true and correct.

Executed on February 26, 1980 ....
at San Jose, California.

7417

**FICTITIOUS BUSINESS NAME
STATEMENT
NO. 53279**
The following person(s) is (are) doing business as: KINGSTONE BEDDING WAREHOUSE, 584 Mayfield Ave., Stanford, CA 94305.
Brett Michael Kingstone, 584 Mayfield Ave., Stanford, CA 94305.
This business is conducted by an individual.
/s/Brett Kingstone
This statement was filed with the County Clerk of Santa Clara County on Jan. 18, 1980.
(Feb: 5,12,19,26)   7417

Figure 7 – Proof of Publication for "DBA"

year license. In June, I will have to pay the full year's fee. The business license also only took about five minutes to complete. Both forms were simple and the people in each department were quite friendly. Once all the forms were filed, I was all ready for business, subject to the pending approval of my zoning permit and business license.

My zoning approval came through in one week. However, I did not receive my city business license until a few months later. The delay in my license was due to the fact a routine fire and safety inspection had to be made by the city before my license was issued.

You should check to see if your city requires any special health permits or consumer protection licenses for your specific business. These licenses are often required for food vendors. Some cities, such as New York City, have special Consumer Protection and Consumer Affairs Agencies which require some businesses to register and/or obtain a special permit. Some states and cities also require special skilled occupational licenses for individuals who wish to sell their services as a contractor, plumber, or repair person, so check your city and state regulations to see if you need an occupational license, if you are selling a specialized skill. A copy of my zoning permit is in Figure 8. A copy of my business license is in Figure 9. I would strongly recommend that you keep a careful file of all your receipts and licenses. You will find it very useful to have them handy in the future. Also they will serve as proof of payment and vouchers for income tax deductions.

Federal Identification Numbers

A social security number is all the identification that you or your business will need with the federal government until you hire employees. Most of you by now probably have a social security number. If you do not you may obtain one by filing form SS-5 with the Social Security Administration. A sample copy of the form filled out for John Doe (who will be used as an example in later tax discussions) is on Figure 10.

If you know in advance that your business is going to hire employees (other than yourself or your business partner) you must file an "Application for Employer Identification Number" form SS-4 with the Internal Revenue Service. If you file for and receive a Federal Employer Identification Number, the IRS will automatically send you quarterly and year-end payroll tax returns which you must complete and return. So don't apply for an employment identification number until you hire an employee. An example of an SS-4 form is shown on Figure 11.

DATE: February 11th, 1980

ZONING CLEARANCE

Name: Brett Kingstone   Use: Warehouse and sales

Address: 4000 Industrial Ave. San Carlos Zoning District: P-M-2

The above is permitted under zoning regulations without any further permit being required.

Architectural approval is/is not required prior to the issuance of any permit under Building Code regulations.

Marhall J. Tore

Signature

The above zoning clearance is subject to the following Standard Conditions:

1. That there shall be such compliance with the building codes and fire regulations as deemed necessary by the building inspector and the fire chief.

2. That prior to the installation of any sign, any needed sign permit shall be secured.

3. That all conditions of the building and fire departments must be met prior to the issuance of any occupancy permit.

4. That any needed business license shall be secured.

5. That the Building Inspector and/or the Fire Marshall shall be responsible for the enforcement of the conditions hereof.

Figure 8 – City Zoning Clearance

CITY OF SAN CARLOS
BUSINESS LICENSE

No. 3344

The person, firm or corporation below named is hereby granted license (pursuant to the provisions of License Ordinance of the City of San Carlos) to engage in carry on or conduct, in the City of San Carlos, the business, trade, calling, profession, exhibition, or avocation described below.

License Fee $ 25.00 ½ y
$ _____
Penalty $ _____
Total $ 25.00 ½ yr

From _1-1-80_ To _6-30-80_

Date Paid _2-13-80_

Owner's Name __ Brett Kingstone __ Phone No. _327 8988_
Address __ 584 Mayfield Ave. Stanford 94305_

Trade Name __ Kingstone Bedding Warehouse (retail store)__

Street _4000 Industrial Ave._   mail to home

City _San Carlos, Calif. 94070_

KEEP THIS LICENSE IN A CONSPICUOUS PLACE

Signed __ *Sadie M. Conboy* __
CITY CLERK

License Not Transferable and Must Be Paid in Advance

Figure 9 – City Business License

DEPARTMENT OF HEALTH AND HUMAN SERVICES
SOCIAL SECURITY ADMINISTRATION

FORM APPROVED
OMB NO. 72-S79002

FORM SS-5 — APPLICATION FOR A
SOCIAL SECURITY NUMBER CARD
(Original, Replacement or Correction)

MICROFILM REF. NO. (SSA USE ONLY)

Unless the requested information is provided, we may not be able to issue a Social Security Number (20 CFR 422.103(b))

INSTRUCTIONS TO APPLICANT — Before completing this form, please read the instructions on the opposite page. You can type or print, using pen with dark blue or black ink. Do not use pencil.

NAME TO BE SHOWN ON CARD: First **JOHN** Middle Last **DOE**

FULL NAME AT BIRTH (IF OTHER THAN ABOVE): First / Middle / Last

OTHER NAME(S) USED:

MAILING ADDRESS (Street/Apt. No., P.O. Box, Rural Route No.) **123 MAIN STREET**

CITY **ANYTOWN** STATE **CALIFORNIA** ZIP CODE **94305**

CITIZENSHIP: [X] a. U.S. citizen

SEX: [X] Male

RACE/ETHNIC DESCRIPTION: [X] e. White (not Hispanic)

DATE OF BIRTH: MONTH **12** DAY **25** YEAR **59** AGE **21** PLACE OF BIRTH CITY **BROOKLYN** STATE OR FOREIGN COUNTRY **NEW YORK**

MOTHER'S NAME AT HER BIRTH: First **RENEE** Middle **JEANETTE** Last (her maiden name) **SILVERS**

FATHER'S NAME: First **LEONARD** Middle **OSCAR** Last **DOE**

a. Have you or someone on your behalf applied for a social security number before? [X] No

TODAY'S DATE: MONTH **1** DAY **1** YEAR **79**

Telephone number where we can reach you during the day: HOME **(415) 555-1212**

WARNING: Deliberately providing false information on this application is punishable by a fine of $1,000 or one year in jail, or both.

YOUR SIGNATURE **John Doe**

YOUR RELATIONSHIP TO PERSON IN ITEM 1: [X] Self

DO NOT WRITE BELOW THIS LINE (FOR SSA USE ONLY)

FORM SS-5 (10-80) PRIOR EDITIONS SHOULD BE DESTROYED

Figure 10 – Form SS-5 Social Security Number

```
                    E.I. NO. 22-1832268        ☆ U.S. GOVERNMENT PRINTING OFFICE : 1979—O-263-409              ▽
```

For clear copy on both parts, please typewrite or print with ball point pen and press firmly   (See Instructions on pages 2 and 4)

Form SS-4 (Rev. 3-79) Department of the Treasury Internal Revenue Service	**Application for Employer Identification Number** (For use by employers and others as explained in the Instructions)	

1 Name (True name as distinguished from trade name. If partnership, see instructions on page 4.)
JOHN DOE

2 Trade name, if any (Name under which business is operated, if different from item 1.) **JOHN'S FURNITURE STORE**	3 Social security number, if sole proprietor **012 34 5678**

4 Address of principal place of business (Number and street) **123 MAIN STREET**	5 Ending month of accounting year **DECEMBER**

6 City and State **ANYTOWN, CALIFORNIA**	7 ZIP code **94305**	8 County of business location **ANYTOWN**

9 Type of organization ☒ Individual ☐ Trust ☐ Partnership ☐ Other (specify) ☐ Governmental (See Instructions on page 4) ☐ Nonprofit organization (See instructions on page 4) ☐ Corporation	10 Date you acquired or started this business (Mo., day, year) **1-1-78**

11 Reason for applying ☐ Started new business ☐ Purchased going business ☒ Other (specify) **HIRED EMPLOYEE**	12 First date you paid or will pay wages for this business (Mo., day, year) **6-1-78**

13 Nature of business (See Instructions on page 4) **RETAIL FURNITURE STORE**	14 Do you operate more than one place of business? ☐ Yes ☒ No

15 Peak number of employees expected in next 12 months (If none, enter "0") ▶ Nonagricultural **I**	Agricultural **O**	Household **O**	16 If nature of business is manufacturing, state principal product and raw material used.

17 To whom do you sell most of your products or services?
☐ Business establishments   ☒ General public   ☐ Other (specify)

18 Have you ever applied for an identification number for this or any other business? ☐ Yes ☒ No
If "Yes," enter name and trade name (if any). ▶
Also enter the approximate date, city, and State where you first applied and previous number if known.

Date **4-1-78**	Signature and title *John Doe* **OWNER**	Telephone number **(415) 555-1212**

Please leave blank ▶	Geo.	Ind.	Class	Size	Reas. for appl.	**Part I**

Figure 11 – Form SS-4 Federal Employer ID Number

Checklist of Requirements

1. State Seller's Permit

2. State Employer's Registration (if you're hiring regular help)

3. County "Doing Business As" Statement

4. City Business License

5. Special Zoning or Occupational Licenses

6. Social Security Number

7. Federal Employer Identification Number

Now that you're a legal business, it's time to get the machinery operating. Start ordering supplies, open a bank account, pass out flyers, and declare yourself open for business. The number of details you'll have to attend to will, of course, depend on the nature and complexity of your business. In the material that follows, I've tried to hit on some of the more basic points. It would be impossible for me to cover all bases for every type of business. Furthermore, as a business grows and changes, its needs will differ. So use what follows as a guideline—ignore what does not apply, add to it, and review it as time goes on. Better yet, read it and make your own detailed list of things to do.

Services and Supplies

Order basic equipment or inventory: T-shirts, balloons, components—whatever. By now you should have some idea of the best suppliers for the materials you need. Try to be realistic about quantities.

Get basic office supplies: ledgers, receipt books, files, etc.

Order printing: business cards, order forms, stationery, etc.

Open bank accounts: (see page 100)

Get telephone service: an answering service will probably cost around $15 to $40 per month. A fairly simple automatic answering machine will cost around $130.

Rent post office box: a small one costs about $10 for six months.

Arrange to rent space: monthly fees for a 5 × 7 × 9-foot high storage shed run around $20. Some of these public storage places have trucks and fork-lifts on the premises. Renting an empty garage is another possibility if you only need storage space. Whatever you rent, don't rely on verbal agreements, and read over rental contracts carefully before signing.

Price your product or service

Pricing starts with what the consumer will pay. This is the number one rule in the real world. The second prime factor is how much it costs you in terms of time and money to provide the goods or services. Finally, you need to know what your competition is charging. No textbook pricing formula will work every time, but there is a systematic way of determining your price.

If you are manufacturing a product, try to estimate the average costs of materials and in the assembly, packaging, and shipping of each unit, then double that figure. If you are a retailer, again, price your product at twice its cost to you. Remember:

Sales Price–Costs of Goods Sold = Gross Profit. Out of this gross profit, you must pay administrative and overhead expenses and, of course, your own salary. The price you arrive at should be one that consumers will be willing to pay (check your competitors' fee schedule now) and that will, at the same time, give you a satisfying return for the money and time you've invested.

Speaking of time, how much do you think your time is worth in dollars per hour? If you are in a service business, you are going to have to determine the value of your time. Whether you're setting up a bicycle repair shop, a resume writing service, a tutoring agency, or a photography studio, you'll have to put a price tag on your service. This will vary according to the type of skill or degree of expertise you have to offer. Here again, you'll need to know what your competitors are charging. (If others are charging $5 per day for housesitting, you'll probably find few takers if you charge $20.) You should also take into account your costs, too, although they will not be the major factor as they are in a manufacturing or retail business. Try to arrive at a price that will make both you and the customer happy.

Advertising

Let's face it. If you want to make money, you've got to make sales, and you won't make sales unless people know that you have something to offer and are interested enough in it to want to buy. The solution to this, in short, is to Advertise, Advertise, Advertise!!!

I am by no means an advertising genius, but here are a few things that I have learned about creating successful advertising:

Direct your advertising specifically to the type of customer you are selling to.

This means catchy phrases for the youngsters and strong assurance of exceptional price and quality for the oldsters. This also means advertise in media that you know will reach your type of customer. An ad for an electric hospital bed just will not do anything for you in a college campus student newspaper.

Be short, sweet and to the point.

Long wordy newspaper advertisements and flyers on bulletin boards just simply won't get read. Use big bold type and get across a few key selling points of your product or service to catch the eye.

Make sure you let them know—who, what, where and when.

After you let them know who you are and what you do, make sure you tell them your address and/or phone number and when they can reach you. This may just seem like common sense, but I've seen many mistakes in this area before, and if you don't let an interested customer know how to reach you, you won't make the sale.

There are many ways that you can sell and advertise your product. It doesn't always require expensive TV and radio advertising to make sales. Here are a few examples:

Newspaper Advertisements: you can place them in school, community, union, or religious newspapers. You can pay as little as $5 for a 4-line classified. In some areas there are throw-away flea-market advertisers.

Flyers: you can design a one-page flyer in either newspaper ad or letter form and distribute them at dormitories, office buildings, apartment buildings, homes, shopping centers, and bulletin boards. Cost for the 1,000 copies might run around $35.

Some advertising material for Kingstone Bedding Warehouse

Telephone solicitation: if you put your private phone on an unlimited local call basis you can call local residents and business owners to your heart's content and tell them about your product or service and ask them for either an order or an appointment. It may sound dumb but most new newspaper and magazine orders and home insulation sales are made through this method of advertising. Write yourself a short catchy sales pitch to catch their interest, then ask them how much they want and when do they want it, at the end of your sales pitch. This approach takes a lot of time and patience, but if you stick to it, it really pays off. Never underestimate the effectiveness of calling people on the telephone. Brett Johnson (Crowd Caps) made most of his initial contacts by making a few well-placed calls.

Door-to-Door Sales: Quite obviously I couldn't go lugging a bed around door-to-door to make sales, but I hear many appliance, Avon, and "Fuller Brush" salespeople do quite well. I did have some experience in selling door-to-door in that after setting appointments with my prospective customers who responded to my flyer, newspaper ads, or telephone calls, I would often transport the adjustable bed to their homes in a rented van and make sales presentations. As I said before, I soon found out that my percentage of sales was much higher when I visited customers at their homes. In fact, all the nationally televised adjustable bed companies sell by sending representatives to the customer's homes. People feel more comfortable at home and it is an environment more conducive to making a sale. Also for the same reason door-to-door would be great for student products. You can also go door-to-door at retail businesses in order to sell your product. Bring a sample, a well-prepared sales pitch, a brochure or two, and a confident attitude.

Use your imagination and keep your eyes, ears, and mind open to new ideas. Try to think up catchy new advertising ideas, and keep on experimenting until you find the most successful methods for your business. Always maintain a positive attitude. Remember, as the boss you are the one who controls your fate and can make things happen. It is your enthusiasm and ambition that will turn your ideas into sales dollars.

Promotions

The general business definition of promotion is "free advertising." Getting some free advertising for your business can be simply a matter of contacting your school and local newspapers. They may be more than happy to write a story about "local entrepreneur makes good." Two of my university's newspapers, the *Stanford Daily* and the *Campus Report*, have run a number of articles about my business (and this book) which led to more sales and business contacts for me.

But don't stop there. Even the big newspapers are accessible in terms of promoting your business idea. After writing this book, I decided to contact the *Wall Street Journal* to try to sell them on the idea of running a story on the new wave of student entrepreneurs. As it turned out, they had me write the story which they printed on their editorial page. What better way to advertise the publication of a new book!

CAMPUS REPORT

Your own small business? Ask Brett Kingstone how!

The Stanford Observer

Student entrepreneurism: healthy and booming

How to succeed in business by trying

THE STANFORD DAILY

Volume 179A, Number 1   Business: 497-2554   Stanford, California   Editorial: 497-4632   Tuesday, June 23, 1981

Students develop a bright idea

THE WALL STREET JOURNAL

From Munchies to Crowd Caps: College Entrepreneurs

"Entrepreneurs are the answer to the American economic problem," claims Brett Johnson, a Harvard junior who is president of Crowd Caps Co., which last year hauled in over six figures in gross sales. On the campus of Baylor University in Waco, Texas, Brent Pennington, a junior majoring in entrepreneurial studies and in-

Manager's Journal

by Brett M. Kingstone

ntor and founder of "Safe-T-Stat," believes that "young entrepreneurs will rejunate the American economy."

Students all over the country are beginning to rediscover just how successful the

Mr. Kingstone, who is graduating from ford University this month, is setting a new business with another Stanford dent to manufacture and market a fiber c lighting system for hotels, casinos supermarkets. His book, "The Student repreneur's Guide," will be published en Speed Press in July.

Q&A With Brett M. Kingstone, student entrepreneur

venture
The Magazine for Entrepreneurs

Hiring Help

If you can possibly do it, try to get along without hiring regular help, because becoming an employer is guaranteed to double your paperwork. You will have to keep payroll records, file extra tax forms (see page xxx), pay additional taxes, and take out insurance. But let's say your business is doing so well that you cannot handle it alone and still keep up with your classwork. In that case, you may have no choice but to hire employees and you might as well go about it in a systematic manner.

First, sit down and write a job description—a list of tasks your new employee will have to do. Then start thinking about the personal qualities you want your help to have—experience, dependability, cooperativeness, industriousness, ability to handle people, etc. Then you start looking for someone who will qualify.

You can go to people you already know. But make sure they want to work and will be willing to deal with you as "the boss." A second possibility is to run classified ads in your school or community newspaper. A third good source are job-listing services at high schools or colleges in your area. These services are free, and they will be happy to hear from you.

One way to avoid the hassles of dealing with permanent employees is to hire independent contractors as you need work done. These people are essentially their own bosses who sell their professional skills to you for a fee. You don't have to keep employment records or pay payroll taxes for them. If you hire specialists to do specific jobs (for instance, an accountant to do your tax work, or a typist to type your contracts and letters), your business will function more smoothly and you won't feel overwhelmed by having to do everything yourself. Often these specialists can do the work much faster and more efficiently than you can and the time you save by hiring them will be more than worth the extra expense.

Insurance

You should analyze whether or not your company needs fire, theft, automobile, or liability insurances. If you have a lot of expensive equipment or tools, don't hesitate. Besides the fact that you want to cover your losses, for a business, this type of insurance is tax deductible. If there are any hazards involved in what you are doing, look into liability insurance so you don't lose your shirt if someone sues you. Rates vary, so contact several insurance brokers before making any decisions.

Copyrights and Patents

If you are publishing any material that you want to protect (for instance if you have written a sports guide, manual, book of poems, etc.) you should copyright it. Contact the Copyright Office, Library of Congress, Washington, D.C. 20559 for filing forms and information. Generally speaking, the procedure is fairly simple. You submit a registration form with a $10 filing fee, and send two copies of your material to the Library of Congress.

Patenting is a more costly and time-consuming matter. The filing fee is $65, and you pay another $100 when the patent is granted. You will also have to pay for a search to determine that your invention is not a duplication of someone else's. This can be quite expensive and the process may take up to two years to complete. However, you should seriously consider going through with it if you have an invention you feel will be valuable.

Should I Incorporate?

Most small businesses in the United States are either sole proprietorships (owned by one person) or partnerships (jointly owned businesses). It seems that most of the owners of small businesses don't feel that it is necessary for them to incorporate. Incorporating a business usually requires at least a few hundred dollars in attorney and filing fees. In addition, a corporation is also more costly and time consuming to maintain than a sole proprietorship and general partnership because there are added corporate income taxes and corporate paperwork requirements (such as writing the minutes of the corporate board of directors meetings which are required by the State).

Then if it is such a pain, why incorporate? Well, one main reason is that by incorporating, your business acquires a separate liability status as a "legal entity." Thus, if your company is sued by a customer or by a bill collector, you and your personal assets cannot be held liable. High risk businesses usually desire the benefits of incorporation. However, your part-time small business enterprise should not be of such "high risk" to require this costly liability protection. Another reason to incorporate is to raise capital for a business by selling stock in the corporation. Here again, part time small businesses should not incorporate because they would usually be better off raising capital by obtaining loans from interested friends or relatives.

If your business starts becoming very profitable and you find yourself approaching the 50% tax bracket on personal income, you may find some benefits from incorporating. These benefits usually are found in rather sophisticated tax deferments which corporations can provide by reinvesting profit or "retaining earnings" and also setting up a personal pension fund for the owner. These tax deferment techniques are complicated and usually require the services of a corporate lawyer to have them executed effectively.

If you feel that you may require the benefits of limited liability or tax deferment that can, in some cases, be provided by a corporation you may wish to explore the possibility of becoming a "Subchapter S Corporation." Small businesses may enjoy special benefits, such as being exempt from double corporate taxation as a "Subchapter S Corporation" in some states. Not all states give such benefits to small business corporations and you should check your local state departments of taxation and license for further information.

In this book, I will not delve into the added licensing and tax requirements for corporations because most of you simply will not need to incorporate. For those who are still curious, I will cite IRS documents in the section on taxation which will provide you with further information. For the most part, a sole proprietorship or partnership should meet your needs.

Administering The Business

Record Keeping and Accounting

Good records are essential for efficient management. Unless you keep an accurate account of expenses and receipts, you'll have no idea of your business' financial status. In any case, when you run a business, you are required by law to maintain records that will enable you to prepare complete and accurate tax returns. You may choose any system suited to the purpose and nature of your business that will clearly establish not only your gross income, but also your deductions and credits. This means you should keep a business checkbook, an income ledger, and an expense ledger, and you should save all data that supports the entries in those records. Paid bills, cancelled checks, sales slips, invoices, bank deposit slips, etc., should all be filed in an orderly manner and stored in a safe place.

Generally, the IRS requires records to be maintained for three years after the return is due to be filed, or two years from the date the tax was paid, whichever occurs later. I would recommend that you keep all receipts for your expensive supplies or property for as long as you own them. These receipts can be used as proof of ownership.

If you are selling a product which is expensive, requires a warranty, or allows for partial payment to be made in the future, I suggest you write up a contract or sales receipt for each item you sell. You should keep a copy (either carbon or photocopy) of this receipt with the date, product sold, purchase price, cash received, cash due, purchaser's address, purchaser's signature, and any special sales agreement or warranty that was made at time of sale. This document will protect both yourself and your customer from any breaches of contract. If your customer owes you money, this may be the only proof you will have of the debt. An example of one of my company's sale receipts is in Figure 12. After the receipt is typed up with a carbon copy and signed by the customer I usually photocopy it along with the down payment and file it in a separate sales file.

Other records that you should carefully keep complete files of are

INVOICE NO. 0771

Kingstone Bedding Warehouse

SOLD TO Mr. McGrayle
Marvin Gardens, Apt. A
Lytton Ave.
Palo Alto, CA 94305

SHIPPED TO
SAME.

QUANTITY	DESCRIPTION	UNIT PRICE	AMOUNT
1	Floral Print Balboa - Flex-a-Bed Display Model	$580	
	Less Display Discount	$550	
	6 1/2% Tax		37.85
	Total Amount Due		$587.85
	Down Payment 3/15/80.................		387.85
	Payment Due on recieval of Merchandise...		$200.00

I understand that a $50 discount will be applied to my second purchase.

I understand that all sales are final and that the bed is under warranty from the manufacturer as expressed in the limited warranty booklet.

Signature

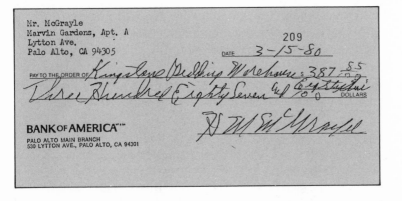

Figure 12 – Sales Receipt with Sales Agreement and Check for Down Payment

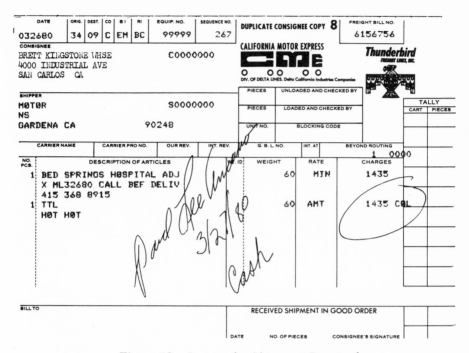

Figure 13 – Invoice for Shipment Received

delivery invoices for merchandise received (shown in Figure 13), signed by warehousemen, and, merchandise delivery invoices signed by customers (shown in Figure 14), and expense receipts for business operations (as shown by my rental agreement receipt for a van used for my business (Figure 15). Remember, these receipts serve as proof of payment, customer receipts, and business expenses.

For more information on record keeping, obtain Publication 583, *Record Keeping For a Small Business*, and Publication 552, *Record Keeping Requirements and a Guide to Tax Publications*, available from your local IRS office.

There are four basic financial records that you must keep in order to maintain a reasonable day-to-day accounting of the financial situation of your business:

1. a business checking account,
2. a business savings account,
3. an expenditure ledger or journal and
4. an income ledger or journal.

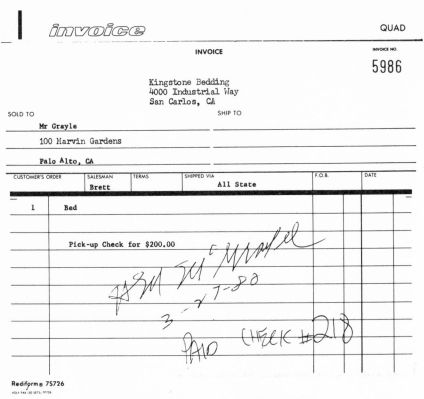

Figure 14 – Invoice for Delivery Made

To maintain these records you do not have to be an economics major or have any great knowledge of accounting. All you have to do is simply put aside the time at the end of each day to record your transactions and make certain the balances and totals are up to date.

Bank Accounts

Your business checking account can be set up at your local bank by filing a copy of your DBA statement with them. Your business check should be printed with the address where you wish your mail or correspondence to be sent. In my case, it was my dorm address but I also gave my home address as well. Your business checks will most probably come in a looseleaf hole punched binder. Each business check will be numbered and attached to a corresponding numbered check stub. You should fill out the date, amount, payee (person or company for whom it is intended) and the purpose of the payment. You must remember to fill out each check stub *immediately* after you write the check, as it is possible to forget the amount or the person paid. This forgetfulness is common in many student checking accounts, but it cannot be tolerated in a business checking account. If

HENGEHOLD MOTOR COMPANY (LESSOR)
762 SAN ANTONIO ROAD
PALO ALTO, CALIFORNIA 94303

RENTAL AGREEMENT
No. 69973

no no il 55. 83

EQUIPMENT NUMBER					CHARGES
10	MAKE *Tord*	MAXIMUM PAYLOAD *2000* LBS	DATE IN	TIME IN	
Econ	BODY TYPE	LICENSE NUMBER *LH8469*	DATE OUT *3-28-80*	TIME OUT *9:—*	

CUSTOMER BILLING — **INVOICE**

HOURS @ =

MILES IN

CUSTOMER NAME: *Kingstone Bedding Warehouse*
ADDRESS: *584 Mayfield ave*
CITY & STATE: *Stanford CA* ZIP

MILES OUT *45839*
TOTAL MILES *45954* @ =

SUB TOTAL

PHONE NUMBER *321-8780* / PURCHASE ORDER NUMBER

LESSOR MAKES NO WARRANTIES: EXPRESS, IMPLIED OR STATUTORY, INCLUDING, BUT NOT LIMITED TO, THE IMPLIED WARRANTIES OF MERCHANTABILITY AND FITNESS FOR A PARTICULAR PURPOSE.
THE VEHICLE DESCRIBED HEREIN IS RENTED PURSUANT TO AND IN ACCORDANCE WITH THE TERMS AND CONDITIONS SET OUT ON BOTH SIDES OF THIS RENTAL AGREEMENT. THIS IS PAGE 2.
CUSTOMER REPRESENTS THAT HE HAS READ BOTH PAGE 1 AND PAGE 2 OF THIS RENTAL AGREEMENT AND AGREES TO THE CONDITIONS THEREOF.

SIGNATURE: X *Brett M. Kingston*
LEASE PRINT NAME: *BRETT KINGSTONE* AGE
DRIVERS LICENSE NUMBER: *N9261980* STATE *CO* EXPIRES / *82*

	NO.		PER DAY
DOLLY	$		PER DAY
			PER DAY
	QTY.	$	PER DAY
COLLISION DAMAGE WAIVER	DAYS ⑤		PER DAY
GASOLINE			GAL.

TERMS: NET 10 DAYS. A FINANCE CHARGE OF 1½% PER MONTH (18% PER ANNUM) WILL BE ADDED TO ALL OVERDUE ACCOUNTS

EMPLOYER: *Above*
ADDRESS:
EMPLOYEE I.D. NO.
WORK PHONE

TOTAL *51.54*

ALL CHARGES ARE SUBJECT TO FINAL AUDIT.
MILEAGE DETERMINED BY READING FACTORY INSTALLED ODOMETER/HUBODOMETER.

	PER MILE	PER DAY	PER WEEK	PER MONTH	OVERTIME	PLUS GAS
RATE	*14¢*	*24* $	$	$	FOUR	

HAULING: *Equip* STREET FROM CITY *1008* PHONE NO.
DEPOSIT: *C.K.* REFUND RECEIVED $ INITIAL FOR REFUND

STREET *San Carlos*
TO CITY *RET*
VEHICLE TO BE RETURNED ON OR BEFORE
DATE *3-30/80* TIME A.M. P.M.

COLLISION DAMAGE WAIVER

By his initial, Customer agrees to pay a charge as specified above per day or fraction of a day and Lessor agrees to waive all claims against Customer for the first $750 of damage by COLLISION to vehicle while it is used, operated or driven in conformity with this Rental Agreement.

WARNING: Whether or not the fee is paid, if the vehicle is used operated or driven in violation of any provision of this Rental Agreement, or is damaged by STRIKING OVERHEAD OBJECTS, or is driven off concrete paved highways, or is damaged by pushing another vehicle or object, or by owning another vehicle or trailer, customer shall be liable for all damage. Customer is also fully liable, at all times, for any tire or inner tube damage and for any damage, of whatever nature, that occurs as a result of loading or unloading the vehicle or any damage caused by improperly secured loads.

DECLINES INITIAL HERE

ACCEPTS INITIAL HERE *BK*

RENTAL AGREEMENT
PREPARED BY *Jon—*
COMPUTED BY

I understand that I bear full liability for damage caused by hitting overhead objects and that Lessor DOES NOT provide any insurance coverage for this.

H.M.C.

- COPY OF RENTAL AGREEMENT MUST BE IN POSSESSION OF DRIVER AT ALL TIMES.
- IF DELAYED IN RETURNING VEHICLE PLEASE CALL IN!
- CUSTOMER RESPONSIBLE FOR ALL PARKING AND TRAFFIC VIOLATIONS.

PAGE 2 – ADDITIONAL TERMS ON REVERSE SIDE HEREOF.

CUSTOMER COPY

Figure 15 – Rental Agreement

you don't keep an orderly record you will not be able to maintain a good understanding of your weekly expenses and profits and you will undoubtedly be bound for trouble. Good record keeping is good business practice. Figure 16 is an example of my business check. A copy of my bank's business checking agreement is shown on Figure 17A.

I would recommend that most, if not all, of your business expenses be paid by check because it serves as a proof of payment: if disputes arise, you will have a cancelled check on hand as proof.

Your business savings account can be set up at your local bank just like your regular personal savings account. Here again, the bank will want to see a copy of your DBA to set up your account. Both my savings and my checking accounts were set up as individual sole owner accounts because my business was a sole proprietorship. If you are setting up a business with one or more partners, the account should list all the partners so that they can write checks and make deposits and withdrawals, too. Listing partners on all such forms serves as a statement of legal joint ownership of the business. Remember that there is a big difference between a legal partner (an owner of a business) and an employee. A partner is someone who is putting in a considerable investment in time, money and management of the business. A partner is entitled to a share of the profits. An employee has no legal ownership of the business and is just paid a salary for services rendered. Figure 17B shows a copy of my bank's depositor agreement.

It is a good idea to open a business savings account with funds not needed in your checking account. In this way you can earn interest on your savings. Remember to keep this account up to date. I strongly suggest that you keep both a separate savings and checking account for your business.

Don't use your personal checking and savings for your business, you

KINGSTONE BEDDING WAREHOUSE
(415) 321-8780
584 MAYFIELD AVE STANFORD CA 94305
4410 AUSTIN BLVD.
ISLAND PARK, NY 11558

NO. 150

_____19____

PAY TO THE
ORDER OF _____ $_____

_____ DOLLARS

BANK OF AMERICA

STANFORD FINANCIAL SQUARE BRANCH
2600 EL CAMINO REAL, PALO ALTO, CA 94306

Figure 16 – Business Check

B. BANK OF AMERICA　　　　**Bank-Depositor Agreement**

Sole Proprietorship or Partnership
_____2/8/80_____
DATE

TO: Bank of America NT&SA

By signing this agreement, I open a ☒CHECKING ☐SAVINGS account with you. I understand that you will handle my deposits according to your arrangements for services of this type.

The publication which you give me as part of this agreement tells me how these services now work. I understand that you will inform me of any changes in these services that affect my rights and obligations as a depositor.

I am doing business under the trade name and style of

_____KINGSTONE BEDDING WAREHOUSE_____and

☒ Certify that I am the SOLE OWNER of this firm.
　or
☐ Certify that we are OWNERS of this firm as COPARTNERS and constitute all of the general partners of the partnership.

OWNER(S) sign below:

1. X _Brett Kingstone_　　3. X SOLE OWNER_____

2. X _____　　4. X _____

You may:

- Pay out funds as indicated on the signature card below. However, you may require all OWNERS' signatures if there are conflicts among the OWNERS.
- Endorse checks for me which you receive for deposit.
- ☒ MAIL ☐ HOLD all my statements and other notices.
- Mail them to me if I don't call for them in 30 days. If they are returned to you undelivered, you may destroy them after 2 years.

I agree that you are not responsible for items lost while not in your possession. You or I can end our banking relationship at any time.

(CK) **KINGSTONE BEDDING WAREHOUSE**　　7-224　　(SV)

_____

ACCOUNT TITLE　　　　　　　　　　　ACCOUNT NUMBER

You may pay out funds with any_____/_____of the signatures below. Checks
　　　　　　　　　　　　　(number)
are to be signed by numbers_____and countersigned by numbers_____.

Authorized signatures: Please indicate Mr., Mrs., Ms., Miss (optional)

1. X _____　　　　4. X _____

2. X _____　　　　5. X _____

3. X _____　　　　6. X _____

TEL-105 12-78 (Rev.)　　　Member F.D.I.C.　　　Customer Copy 2

Figure 17A – Bank-Depositor Agreement (Checking)

BA BANK OF AMERICA

Bank-Depositor Agreement

Individual, Joint Tenant, or Trustee

3-18-80

DATE

TO: Bank of America NT&SA

By signing this agreement, I open a ☐ CHECKING ☒ SAVINGS account with you. I understand that you will handle my deposits according to your arrangements for services of this type.

The publication which you give me as part of this agreement tells me how these services now work. I understand that you will inform me of any changes in these services that affect my rights and obligations as a depositor.

I want my account to be: (check one)

☒ INDIVIDUAL (mine alone)

☐ JOINT TENANCY (with one or more persons who have right of survivorship)

☐ TRUSTEE (acting on my own or with others for a beneficiary)

You may:

- Pay out funds with any ____/____ of the signatures below — if I choose a JOINT account. However, you may require all our signatures if there are conflicts among us.
  (number)

- Pay out funds with my signature — if I choose an INDIVIDUAL account.

- Endorse checks for me which you receive for deposit.

- Cash and deposit all checks payable to any signer of this agreement when endorsed by any of us or one for the other.

- ☒ MAIL ☐ HOLD all my statements and other notices.

- Mail them to me if I don't call for them in 30 days. If they are returned to you undelivered, you may destroy them after 2 years.

I agree that you are not responsible for items lost while not in your possession.

Should any of us die or be incapacitated, the other signers agree to notify you in writing immediately.

You or I can end our banking relationship at any time.

(CK)

KINGSTONE, Brett dba
KINGSTONE BEDDING WAREHOUSE   1183-2955

_____

ACCOUNT NAME(S)   ACCOUNT NUMBER

You may pay out funds with any ____/____ of the signatures below — if I choose a
JOINT account.   (number)

Signatures: Please indicate Mr., Mrs., Miss, Ms. (optional)

1. X *Brett Kingstone*

2. X

3. X

TEL-100 8-79   Member F.D.I.C.   Customer Copy 2

Figure 17B – Bank-Depositor Agreement (Savings)

won't be able to maintain a clear record of your business expenses and revenues. Keep all your business records up to date and separate from your personal records. Only then will you be able to get a clear picture of how your business is doing.

Ledgers

Now that you have set up your business checking and business savings accounts you should maintain a separate daily record of all your daily cash expenditures and receipts. For beginners who are unfamiliar with accounting, the simplest method of recording your expenditures and receipts is to maintain a single entry accounting expenditure and income ledger.

See Figure 18 for an example of a typical single entry expenditure ledger. The first line has been filled out as an example. You are to fill in the date of payment, the check number, the total amount paid, and the payee's name. You then fill out the amount of the expenditure under the type of expense it represents. For example, my first business expense was for a county DBA statement which was recorded as a "tax and license" expense since it was payment for a business license. By keeping a separate record of each type of expense you will not only be able to compare your total expenditures, but you will see how your money is being spent. This will give you a good idea of what expenditures might have to be cut back or "watched" in the future.

The income ledger shown in Figure 19, is a record of all your income or sales. The first line is filled out as an example. In my income ledger I fill in the date, the sale amount, the sales tax, the cash received at time of sale, the amount due on delivery and the total sales amount. Since I generally collect 60 percent in advance, and 40 percent on delivery of the bed to the customer, I need to keep a separate record of my cash received from my cash due. In a "cash and carry" business, such as a cookie business where the full amount is paid at the time of the sale, you will not need to complete the separate cash received and payment due accounts.

It is important to know the separate amounts for sales, cash received, and accounts receivable (money owed to your business) because this gives you an accurate account of the financial condition of your business. If you made $100 in sales and have only $50 in expenses, your business might seem to be doing alright. But if it turns out that out of the $100 in sales you have received only $30 in cash and the remaining balance is owed to you, you are in trouble because you have spent more than you have on hand and this may mean a bounced check or digging into your personal funds again.

	Initials	Date
Prepared By		
Approved By		

EXPENDITURE LEDGER FOR THE MONTH OF JANUARY

	DATE CHECK #	PAYEE	Total	Inventory	Supplies	Labor	Advertising
			1	2	3	4	5
1	1/18/80 001	Santa Clara County	10 00				
2							
3							
4							
5							
6							
7							
8							
9							
10							
11							
12							
13							
14							
15							
16							
17							
18							
19							
20							
21							
22							
23							
24							
25							
26							
27							
28							
29							
30							
31							
32							
33							
34							
35							
36							
37							
38							
39							
40							

Figure 18 – Expenditure Ledger

	Initials	Date
Prepared By		
Approved By		

EXPENDITURE LEDGER FOR THE MONTH OF JANUARY

		1	2	3	4	5
	Continued	Rent	Utilities	Tax & Licenses	Education	Other
1				10 00		
2						
3						
4						
5						
6						
7						
8						
9						
10						
11						
12						
13						
14						
15						
16						
17						
18						
19						
20						
21						
22						
23						
24						
25						
26						
27						
28						
29						
30						
31						
32						
33						
34						
35						
36						
37						
38						
39						
40						

Figure 18 – Continued

	Initials	Date
Prepared By		
Approved By		

INCOME LEDGER FOR THE MONTH OF MARCH

			1	2	3	4	5
	DATE	CUSTOMER	Taxable Sales	Sales Tax	Cash Received	Payment Due	Total Sales
1	3/15/80	McGrayel	550 00	37 85	387 85	200 00	550 00
2							
3							
4							
5							
6							
7							
8							
9							
10							

Figure 19 – Income Ledger

Neither is appealing once you get your business going. It is better to keep a sharp eye on expenses and on cash received and owed. Having enough cash on hand to meet expenses is called having "liquidity." Any business man will tell you that a business that is "illiquid" (not having liquidity) is bound for trouble.

Be sure to make weekly checks of your total expenses and income. Your profits are measured as:

$$\text{Profits} = \text{Total Income} - \text{Total Expenses}$$

Remember also to check to see if you have enough cash on hand to pay your bills. If you don't you should either hustle and make a few more sales, collect some payments that are due, start requiring your customers to pay a larger percentage of their purchase in advance, or simply raise your prices. This is basically the same analysis that most full time big businesses use to check their profits and decide on possible changes in sales volume, payment policy, and price strategy.

You can usually buy this type of ledger or "accounting worksheet" paper at most stationery stores. The titles of all the expenditure and income categories may not be filled out on these ledgers so you can use the exhibits as models. You may decide to make your own additional headings for accounts. For example, I added a separate account for education expense because I often paid for my economics books and part of my tuition expenses out of my business. After all, the United States Treasury Regulation 1,162-5 states that all education expenses commensurate with "improving professional skills" are tax deductible business expenses. Here lies another advantage of running your own business which will be discussed in the next part of this section on taxes.

If you wish information on more sophisticated accounting for your business, I suggest that you consult a standard college accounting text which will show you the "double entry accounting system" and how to prepare a balance sheet and income statement. These statements will give you an even better picture of the financial condition of the business.

Taxes

Now we come to a subject that normally scares the hell out of most of our parents and confuses most students. If you are not already a taxpayer, you probably know little or nothing about taxes. You probably have the impres-

BT-401-AC3 FRONT REV. 9 (1-79)   P O BOX 26100
STATE OF CALIFORNIA   SAN JOSE CA 95159
BOARD OF EQUALIZATION – Department of Business Taxes

STATE, LOCAL and DISTRICT SALES and USE TAX RETURN

DUE ON OR BEFORE	APR. 30, 1980	FOR JAN THROUGH MAR 1980 PERIOD YEAR

Mail to:

KINGSTONE BEDDING WAREHOUSE
BRETT MICHAEL KINGSTONE
584 MAYFIELD AVENUE
STANFORD   CA   94305

PARTIAL PERIOD   29 4300 01/80 D

BUSINESS CODE   SY X 20   AREA CODE   6   ACCOUNT NUMBER   SY GH 20-643724

NAME   **WORK COPY**

BUSINESS ADDRESS   Not acceptable as a Return by the

CITY   State Board of Equalization   REPORTING BASIS

STATE SALES AND USE TAX   READ INSTRUCTIONS BEFORE PREPARING

1. TOTAL SALES .... IF YOU INCLUDE TAX CHARGED – SEE LINE 9	$ 1,280.00
2. ADD—Purchase price of tangible personal property purchased without California sales or use tax and used for some purpose other than resale ENTER "NONE" IF YOU HAVE NOTHING TO REPORT	NONE
3. TOTAL (Line 1 plus Line 2) ...... ENTER "NONE" IF YOU HAVE NOTHING TO REPORT	$ 1,280.00
DEDUCT EXEMPT TRANSACTIONS (See Instructions)	
4. Sales to other retailers for purposes of resale .... $ NONE	
5. Nontaxable Sales of Food Products .... "	
6. Nontaxable Labor (Repair and Installation) .... "	
7. Sales to the United States Government .... "	
8. Sales in interstate or foreign commerce to out-of-state consumers ..... "	
9. Amount of sales tax (if any) included in Line 1 .... "	
10. Other exempt transactions (See Instruction 10) .... "	
11. TOTAL TRANSACTIONS EXEMPT FROM STATE & COUNTY SALES & USE TAX (Lines 4 thru 10)	NONE
12. Amount on which STATE & COUNTY Sales and Use Tax applies (Line 3 minus Line 11)	$ 1,280.00
13. AMOUNT OF TAX .... 5% (4¾% State, ¼% County) (Multiply amount on Line 12 by .05)	$ 64.00

UNIFORM LOCAL SALES AND USE TAX

14. Amount on which State Tax applies (Enter amount from Line 12)	$ 1,280.00
15. ADD—Other local tax adjustments (See Instruction 15)	NONE
16. TOTAL (Line 14 plus Line 15)	$ 1,280.00
17. DEDUCT—Transactions exempt from local tax only (See Instruction 17)	NONE
18. Amount on which LOCAL Tax applies (Line 16 minus Line 17)	$ 1,280.00
19. AMOUNT OF LOCAL TAX 1% (Multiply amount on Line 18 by .01)	$ 12.80

DISTRICT SALES AND USE TAX

20a. Amount of San Francisco Bay Area Rapid Transit District Tax (From Line A12 Column A of Schedule A) a	$ NONE
20b. Amount of Santa Clara County Transit District Tax (From Line A12 Column B of Schedule A) d	$ 6.40
20c. Amount of Santa Cruz Metropolitan Transit District Tax (From Line A12 Column C of Schedule A) e	$ NONE

TOTAL TAX

21. TOTAL STATE, COUNTY, LOCAL & DISTRICT TAX (Total of Lines 13, 19, 20a, 20b & 20c) TOTAL TAX	$ 83.20
22. Deduct amount of sales or use tax or reimbursement therefor imposed by other states and paid by you on the purchase of tangible personal property. Purchase price must be included in Line 2. (See Instruction 22)	NONE
23. NET STATE, COUNTY, LOCAL AND DISTRICT TAX (Line 21 minus Line 22)	$ 83.20
24. LESS—Tax Prepayments 1ST MONTH NONE 2ND MONTH NONE Total Prepayments	NONE
25. REMAINING STATE, COUNTY, LOCAL AND DISTRICT TAX (Line 23 minus Line 24)	$ 83.20
26. Penalty of 10% (.10) if payment is made after the due date shown above ... Penalty	NONE
27. Interest of 1% (.01) per month or part of a month if payment is made after above due date ... Interest	NONE
28. **TOTAL AMOUNT DUE AND PAYABLE** (Line 25 plus Lines 26 & 27)	$ 83.20

I hereby certify that this return, including any accompanying schedules and statements, has been examined by me and to the best of my knowledge and belief is a true, correct and complete return.

SIGNATURE AND TITLE   *Brett Kingstone, Owner*   (415) 885-5282   PHONE NUMBER

MAKE CHECK OR MONEY ORDER PAYABLE TO STATE BOARD OF EQUALIZATION

Figure 20 – State Sales Tax Return

;30 FRONT REV. 8(5-79)
HEDULE C - DETAILED ALLOCATION BY
   SUBOUTLET OF UNIFORM LOCAL SALES AND USE TAX

STATE OF CALIFORNIA
BOARD OF EQUALIZATION
DEPARTMENT OF BUSINESS TAXES

THE ORIGINAL COPY OF THIS SCHEDULE MUST BE ATTACHED TO YOUR RETURN.

READ INSTRUCTIONS BEFORE PREPARING

TAXING JURISDICTION IN WHICH BUSINESS ESTABLISHMENTS ARE LOCATED COL. 1	Sub-outlet Number	TAX AREA CODE COL. 2	AMOUNT OF 1% LOCAL TAX COL. 3
000 Industrial Way SAN CARLOS	002	4120	*NONE*
		*	
84 MAYFIELD AVE. STANFORD	001	4398	$12.80
		*	

Figure 20 – Continued

SCHEDULE A – COMPUTATION SCHEDULE FOR DISTRICT SALES AND USE TAX
PLEASE READ INSTRUCTIONS BEFORE PREPARING THIS SCHEDULE. REVERSE CARBON BEFORE MAKING ENTRIES.

This schedule is to be completed for District Sales and Use Tax on transactions (1) when your business is located in a transit district imposing such taxes and/or (2) you are engaged in business in a transit district and are required to collect the district tax on sales, or leases which are subject to the district use tax.

A1. Amount on which LOCAL Tax applies. (Enter amount from Line 18 on the reverse side)	$	1,280.00
A2. DEDUCT—Amount of transactions (sales) not subject to district sales or use tax made from locations outside transit district(s)	$	NONE
A3. Amount of transit district transactions (Line A1 minus Line A2)	$	1,280.00

ALLOCATE TOTAL ON LINE A3 TO PROPER TRANSIT DISTRICT(S) ON LINE A4	SAN FRANCISCO BAY AREA COLUMN A	DISTRICT SANTA CLARA COUNTY COLUMN B	SANTA CRUZ COUNTY COLUMN C
A4. Enter amount from Line A3 allocated to the proper transit district(s) (Total of this line must equal Line A3 above)	$	$ 1,280.00	$
A5. ADD—Other DISTRICT Tax adjustments (See Instruction A5)		NONE	
A6. TOTAL—(Line A4 plus Line A5)	$	$ 1,280.00	$
DEDUCT EXEMPT TRANSACTIONS (See Instruction A7-9)			
A7. Sales of property shipped to a point outside the district for use elsewhere in California	$	$ NONE	$
A8. Sales made under a fixed price contract or a fixed price lease executed prior to the effective date of the DISTRICT Tax	$	$ "	$
A9. Other exempt transactions or adjustments	$	$ "	$
A10. Total Transactions Exempt from the DISTRICT Tax (Lines A7 through A9)	$	$ 1,280.00	$
A11. Amount on which the DISTRICT Tax applies (Line A6 minus Line A10)	$	$ 6.40	$
A12. Amount of ½% DISTRICT Tax (Multiply amount on Line A11 by .005)			

On reverse side, enter amount from Line A12 on: Line 20a   Line 20b   Line 20c

SCHEDULE B – DETAILED ALLOCATION BY COUNTY OF 1% UNIFORM LOCAL SALES AND USE TAX
PLEASE READ INSTRUCTIONS BEFORE PREPARING THIS SCHEDULE. REVERSE CARBON BEFORE MAKING ENTRIES.
The 1% uniform local sales and use tax on retail sales of merchandise (not involving installation) made at your permanent place of business in California or local tax on property purchased ex-tax and used at this place of business, should be entered on Line B2 below the county schedule. Enter 1% local tax on all other transactions in Column C of the schedule after the name of the county where the sale or use occurred.

A	B	C	A	B	C	A	B	C	A	B	C
COUNTY IN WHICH	C O D	AMOUNT OF 1% LOCAL TAX	COUNTY IN WHICH TAXABLE TR	C O	AMOUNT OF TAX	COUNTY IN WHICH TAXABLE TRANSACTION	C O	AMOUNT OF	COUNTY IN WHICH TAXABLE TRANSACTION RRED	C O D E	AMOUNT OF 1% LOCAL TAX

Figure 20 – Continued

sion that they are very complicated and confusing. In actuality, if you simply take the time to read the federal and state tax booklets, you will find that neither is true. If you have kept good accounting records of your income and expenses, as described, it should take a very short time to complete each of the federal and state tax forms.

State Sales Tax
 The tax that you will probably be paying most frequently is the sales tax. Basically, the sales tax represents an additional charge on each item you sell which you must collect and set aside for payment to your State Board of Equalization or State Revenue Office. They will send you the sales tax forms to complete and notify you when payment is due.
 Your taxes may differ according to what county and state your business is operating in. In some counties, in addition to a county and state sales tax, an additional public transit or public project sales tax may be assigned.
 For the sales I made in San Mateo County, I was required to collect 6% sales taxes and for the sales I made in Santa Clara County, I was required to collect 6.5% sales taxes. To give you an idea of the distribution of these taxes, out of the total 6.5% sales tax paid in Santa Clara County 4¾% goes to the state, ¼% goes to the county, 1% goes to the local city or town and ½% goes to the Santa Clara County Transit District. All the specific tax amounts are filled out on the sales tax form. When you mail your check for the total sum to the State Board of Equalization headquarters in Sacramento, they handle all the disbursements. This state sales tax form is easy to complete, and a copy of it is shown in Figure 20.
 As you can see, all my sales taxes were from Santa Clara County because my first sales were from a brochure rather than my warehouse when I was just starting out selling in late February. For tax purposes, I recorded sales only after the merchandise was delivered and the full payment amount was received. This helped my cash flow.

Federal Business Taxes
 Certain forms must be filed with the federal government if your total combined wages, interest, and part-time business income exceeds $3,300 for the year. The following explanation of federal business taxes has been, for a large part, taken directly from the Internal Revenue Service Publication 1066 (Rev. 5–79), *Small Business Tax Workbook*. This workbook is available free of charge at your local IRS office. It gives a clear concise description of federal business income taxes and I would strongly recom-

mend that you pick up a copy. A detailed description of federal income taxes is also provided in IRS Publication 17, *Your Federal Income Tax*.

The purpose of this section is to give you a general idea how to:

1. determine net profit or loss for your business,
2. know what tax returns and schedules relate to your business,
3. determine liability for estimated tax payments and self-employment tax,
4. determine tax advantages for business persons.

This section is by no means a complete and exhaustive discussion of all the federal tax forms and requirements. A "complete" discussion would no doubt fill an encyclopedia. However, I have endeavored to familiarize you with the most commonly used forms. I have also cited within this section many IRS publications which you can refer to for more detailed information. As your business grows and becomes more sophisticated you may later want to obtain the advice and assistance of an accountant. Very often hiring an accountant to do your paperwork can prevent headaches, and give you more free time to build up your business.

Federal Income Tax

In order to prepare your Federal income tax return, you will need to understand the basic steps for determining your business' profit or loss. This procedure is fairly simple and is much the same for each type of business organization. Basically, profit or loss is determined as follows:

$$\text{Income} - \text{Expenses} = \text{Profit (Loss)}$$

You will use this formula with some slight changes in determining your profit or loss on your tax return. Figure 21 explains the determination of profit or loss and distribution of income for the different types of business organizations.

Gross receipts or sales are the income a business takes in. For example, let's say John decided to start a part-time antique furniture store in his home on weekends. John's Furniture Store sold $4,600 worth of furniture in its first year. Therefore, John's Furniture Store had $4,600 in gross receipts or sales.

Cost of goods sold (sales) is the cost to the business to buy or make

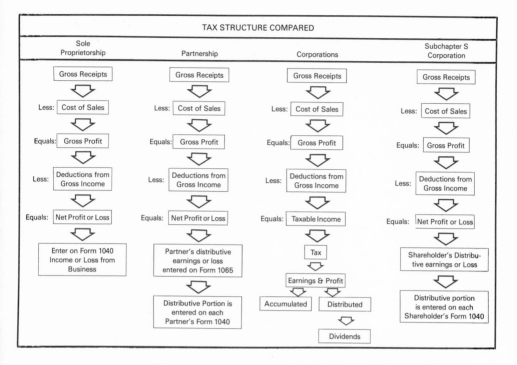

Figure 21 – Business Tax Structure Chart

the product to sell to the consumer. It would be simple to figure the cost of sales if you sold all your merchandise during the year. However, this seldom happens. Some of the sales during the year will probably be from inventory carried over from a prior year. To determine the cost of sales when you have an ending inventory you add the cost of goods purchased during the year to the value of inventory on hand at the beginning of the year. From this total you subtract the value of your inventory at the end of the year. For example, John's Furniture Store purchased $2,000 of furniture from a manufacturer during the year. The store had $1,000 worth of furniture on hand at the beginning of the year for a total of $3,000. From this total they subtracted the value of their ending inventory, $800, so the cost of goods sold is $2,200.

Beginning Inventory + Purchases − Ending Inventory =
Cost of sales

Gross profit is the gross receipts less the cost of goods sold. John's Furniture Store had gross receipts of $4,600; the cost to John for the furniture sold was $2,200; the gross profit was $2,400. Business expenses are the ordinary and necessary expenses incurred in the operation of the business. John's Furniture Store incurred $600 for the salesperson's salaries and $600 for building expenses, supplies, etc.

Profit is the amount by which income of a period exceeds the expenses (cost of goods sold and operating expenses) of the same period. Net loss is the amount by which the expenses exceed the income. John's Furniture Store had sales of $4,600; cost of goods sold of $2,200; and operating expenses of $1,200, leaving John's Furniture Store with a profit of $1,200.

Since a student operated part-time small business will usually not need to incorporate, (or want to deal with the extra corporate tax and paperwork hassles), I will only discuss income taxes for sole proprietorships and partnerships. If you want information on corporate taxes consult IRS Publication 542 *Corporations and the Federal Income Tax* and IRS Publication 589, *Tax Information on Subchapter S Corporations*. Publication 589 specializes in showing corporate taxes for small corporations. Figure 21 provides a chart which illustrates the different types of tax structures for sole proprietorships, partnerships, and corporations.

Please refer now to Schedule C (Form 1040), Figure 22, if you are a sole proprietor; Form 1065, Figure 23 if you are a partnership. The reverse side of Schedule C (Form 1040), that is, page 2, is for assisting you in your calculations.

The first entry related to income at the top of each form is gross receipts or gross sales. Next, cost of goods sold is deducted to determine gross profit. Your form may list several types of income which can be added to gross profit to determine total income.

On Schedule C line 2 and Schedule C–1 line 8 the federal government tax forms combine the cost of goods sold and operating expenses into a figure called "cost of goods sold and/or operations." This sum subtracted from John's sales of $4,600 leaves us again with a profit figure for John which was shown earlier of $1,200. This amount is entered on line 3 of Schedule C.

On line 3 of Schedule C the profit figure is referred to as "gross profit." This added to line 4 "other income" (provided you have any) is listed on line 5 as total income. Other income generally refers to miscellaneous business income such as income from a sale of part of your business. The IRS provides separate schedules for other income and you can obtain them from your local IRS office. From the figure for total income on line 5 you can now make deductions for business related expenses. Your total income minus your business expenses will give you your net profit.

116   *Administering the Business*

SCHEDULE C (Form 1040) — Department of the Treasury, Internal Revenue Service

Profit or (Loss) From Business or Profession (Sole Proprietorship)
Partnerships, Joint Ventures, etc., Must File Form 1065.
▶ Attach to Form 1040 or Form 1041. ▶ See Instructions for Schedule C (Form 1040).

1979 — 09

Name of proprietor: **JOHN DOE**
Social security number of proprietor: **012 34 5678**

A. Main business activity (see Instructions) ▶ **RETAILER**; product ▶ **FURNITURE**
B. Business name ▶ **JOHN'S FURNITURE STORE**
C. Employer identification number: **79 1234516**
D. Business address (number and street) ▶ **123 MAIN ST.**
City, State and Zip Code ▶ **ANYTOWN, CALIFORNIA 94305**
E. Accounting method: (1) ☐ Cash (2) ☒ Accrual (3) ☐ Other (specify) ▶
F. Method(s) used to value closing inventory:
(1) ☒ Cost (2) ☐ Lower of cost or market (3) ☐ Other (if other, attach explanation)
G. Was there any major change in determining quantities, costs, or valuations between opening and closing inventory? — No ✓. If "Yes," attach explanation.
H. Did you deduct expenses for an office in your home? — No ✓
I. Did you elect to claim amortization (under section 191) or depreciation (under section 167(o)) for a rehabilitated certified historic structure (see Instructions)? — No ✓
(Amortizable basis (see Instructions) ▶)

Part I — Income

1a Gross receipts or sales	1a	4,600 00	
b Returns and allowances	1b	NONE	
c Balance (subtract line 1b from line 1a)	1c	4,600 00	
2 Cost of goods sold and/or operations (Schedule C–1, line 8)	2	3,400 00	
3 Gross profit (subtract line 2 from line 1c)	3	1,200 00	
4 Other income (attach schedule)	4		
5 Total income (add lines 3 and 4) ▶	5	1,200 00	

Part II — Deductions

6 Advertising		31a Wages	
7 Amortization		b Jobs credit	
8 Bad debts from sales or services		c WIN credit	
9 Bank charges	50 00	d Total credits	
10 Car and truck expenses		e Subtract line 31d from 31a	
11 Commissions		32 Other expenses (specify):	
12 Depletion		a EDUCATIONAL	100 00
13 Depreciation (explain in Schedule C–2)	260 00	b	
14 Dues and publications	20 00	c	
15 Employee benefit programs		d	
16 Freight (not included on Schedule C–1)		e	
17 Insurance		f	
18 Interest on business indebtedness		g	
19 Laundry and cleaning		h	
20 Legal and professional services		i	
21 Office supplies		j	
22 Pension and profit-sharing plans		k	
23 Postage		l	
24 Rent on business property		m	
25 Repairs		n	
26 Supplies (not included on Schedule C–1)		o	
27 Taxes		p	
28 Telephone	30 00	q	
29 Travel and entertainment		r	
30 Utilities	50 00	s	

33 Total deductions (add amounts in columns for lines 6 through 32s) ▶ **33** — **510 00**
34 Net profit or (loss) (subtract line 33 from line 5). If a profit, enter on Form 1040, line 13, and on Schedule SE, Part II, line 5a (or Form 1041, line 6). If a loss, go on to line 35. **34** — **690 00**
35 If you have a loss, do you have amounts for which you are not "at risk" in this business (see Instructions)? ☐ Yes ☐ No

283-062-1

Figure 22 – Schedule C Profit (Loss) Statement (Sole Proprietorship)

Schedule C (Form 1040) 1979 — Page 2

SCHEDULE C–1.—Cost of Goods Sold and/or Operations (See Schedule C Instructions for Part I, line 2)

1 Inventory at beginning of year (if different from last year's closing inventory, attach explanation) .	1	1,000 00
2 a Purchases	2a	2,000 00
b Cost of items withdrawn for personal use	2b	NONE
c Balance (subtract line 2b from line 2a)	2c	2000 00
3 Cost of labor (do not include salary paid to yourself)	3	600 00
4 Materials and supplies	4	600 00
5 Other costs (attach schedule)	5	NONE
6 Add lines 1, 2c, and 3 through 5	6	4,200 00
7 Inventory at end of year	7	800 00
8 Cost of goods sold and/or operations (subtract line 7 from line 6). Enter here and on Part I, line 2 . ▶	8	3,400 00

SCHEDULE C–2.—Depreciation (See Schedule C Instructions for line 13)
If you need more space, please use Form 4562.

Description of property (a)	Date acquired (b)	Cost or other basis (c)	Depreciation allowed or allowable in prior years (d)	Method of computing depreciation (e)	Life or rate (f)	Depreciation for this year (g)
1 Total additional first-year depreciation (do not include in items below)——————————————▶						
2 Other depreciation:						
Buildings						
Furniture and fixtures . . .						
Transportation equipment . .						
Machinery and other equipment .						
Other (specify)						
PERSONAL CAR AT 20% BUSINESS USE	1/1/79	7,000	0	STRAIGHT LINE	5	1,300×.20 =$260 00
3 Totals					3	260 00
4 Depreciation claimed in Schedule C–1					4	
5 Balance (subtract line 4 from line 3). Enter here and on Part II, line 13 . . . . ▶					5	260 00

SCHEDULE C–3.—Expense Account Information (See Schedule C Instructions for Schedule C–3)

Enter information for yourself and your five highest paid employees. In determining the five highest paid employees, add expense account allowances to the salaries and wages. However, you don't have to provide the information for any employee for whom the combined amount is less than $25,000, or for yourself if your expense account allowance plus line 34, page 1, is less than $25,000.

Name (a)	Expense account (b)	Salaries and wages (c)
Owner		
1		
2		
3		
4		
5		

Did you claim a deduction for expenses connected with:	Yes	No
A Entertainment facility (boat, resort, ranch, etc.)?		✓
B Living accommodations (except employees on business)?		✓
C Conventions or meetings you or your employees attended outside the U.S. or its possessions? (See Instructions) . .		✓
D Employees' families at conventions or meetings?		✓
If "Yes," were any of these conventions or meetings outside the U.S. or its possessions?		✓
E Vacations for employees or their families not reported on Form W–2?		✓

☆ U.S. GOVERNMENT PRINTING OFFICE 1979—O—283-254 95-0875140

Figure 22 – Continued

Form **1065**	**U.S. Partnership Return of Income** For calendar year 1979,	**1979**
Department of the Treasury Internal Revenue Service	or fiscal year beginning _____, 1979, and ending _____, 19___	

A Principal business activity (see page 12 of Instructions)	**Use IRS label.**	Name JOHN DOE & FRIEND	**D** Employer identification no.
B Principal product or service (see page 12 of Instructions)	**Otherwise please print or type.**	Number and street 123 MAIN ST.	**E** Date business started
C Business code number (see page 12 of Instructions)		City or town, State, and ZIP code ANYTOWN, CALIFORNIA 94305	**F** Enter total assets from Schedule L, line 13, column (D). $

G Check method of accounting:
  (1) ☐ Cash   (2) ☐ Accrual   (3) ☐ Other (attach explanation)

H Is this a final return? ☐ Yes   ☐ No

IMPORTANT—You must fill in all lines and schedules. If more space is needed, see page 2 of Instructions. Enter any items specially allocated to the partners on Schedule K, line 16, and not on the numbered lines on this page or in Schedules A through J.

Income

1a	Gross receipts or sales $ .... 1b Less returns and allowances $ .... Balance ▶	1c	
2	Cost of goods sold and/or operations (Schedule A, line 34)	2	
3	Gross profit (subtract line 2 from line 1c)	3	
4	Ordinary income (loss) from other partnerships and fiduciaries (attach statement)	4	
5	Nonqualifying dividends	5	
6	Interest	6	
7	Net income (loss) from rents (Schedule H, line 2)	7	
8	Net income (loss) from royalties (attach schedule)	8	
9	Net farm profit (loss) (attach Schedule F (Form 1040))	9	
10	Net gain (loss) (Form 4797, line 11)	10	
11	Other income (attach schedule)	11	
12	**TOTAL** income (loss) (combine lines 3 through 11)	12	

Deductions

13a	Salaries and wages (other than to partners) $ .... 13b Less Jobs Credit $ .... Balance ▶	13c	
14	Guaranteed payments to partners (see page 4 of Instructions)	14	
15	Rent	15	
16	Interest	16	
17	Taxes	17	
18	Bad debts (see page 5 of Instructions)	18	
19	Repairs	19	
20	Depreciation (Schedule J, line 5)	20	
21	Amortization (attach schedule)	21	
22	Depletion (other than oil and gas, attach schedule—see page 5 of Instructions)	22	
23a	Retirement plans, etc. (see page 5 of Instructions). (Enter number of plans ▶ ....) . .	23a	
23b	Employee benefit programs (see page 5 of Instructions)	23b	
24	Other deductions (attach schedule)	24	
25	**TOTAL** deductions (add lines 13c through 24)	25	
26	Ordinary income (loss) (subtract line 25 from line 12)	26	

Schedule A—COST OF GOODS SOLD AND/OR OPERATIONS (See Page 3 of Instructions)

27	Inventory at beginning of year (if different from last year's closing inventory, attach explanation) . .	27	
28a	Purchases $ .... 28b Less cost of items withdrawn for personal use $ .... Balance ▶	28c	
29	Cost of labor	29	
30	Materials and supplies	30	
31	Other costs (attach schedule)	31	
32	Total of lines 27 through 31	32	
33	Inventory at end of year	33	
34	Cost of goods sold (subtract line 33 from line 32). Enter here and on line 2, above	34	

Under penalties of perjury, I declare that I have examined this return, including accompanying schedules and statements, and to the best of my knowledge and belief, it is true, correct, and complete. Declaration of preparer (other than taxpayer) is based on all information of which preparer has any knowledge.

Please Sign Here

▶ _____
Signature of general partner

▶ _____
Date

Paid Preparer's Information	Preparer's signature and date ▶		Check if self-employed ▶ ☐	Preparer's social security no.
	Firm's name (or yours, if self-employed) and address ▶		E.I. No. ▶	
			ZIP code ▶	

283–091–2

Figure 23 – Form 1065 Partnership Return of Income

Once you have determined total income, you must deduct business expenses. The expenses (deductions) section of your return lists several of the more common business expenses. In this section, simply enter the total expenses for the tax year on the proper line. The total of these expenses is subtracted from total income to arrive at net profit (loss), ordinary income (loss) or taxable income, depending on which form you are required to use.

For example, if you incurred $50 in gasoline expenses during the year to drive to and from your office or your customers, you may deduct it from your taxable income. Likewise, your Wall Street Journal subscription (or any business publication you receive), your telephone bill for calls to your customers, and your office, your electricity and heating expenses are all deductible. The costs of these services are filled out in the deductions column in Part II of Schedule C for "Car and Truck expenses," "Dues and Publications," "telephone" and "utilities" respectively.

If you do your own accounting for your business, you can also take deductions for any accounting courses and textbooks that you pay for while operating the business. For example, in Part II of the Schedule C, I added a column called "Educational" expenses which I used to illustrate how you can make a deduction for a business course.

If you are using any type of depreciable item such as a machine or a car for your business, you may take an income tax depreciation deduction of that item. For example, if you are using your car solely for business purposes and it was purchased new on the first working day in January for $7,000, assuming it has a five-year useful life and salvage value of $500, a full year's depreciation on it is $1,300—$7,000 minus $500 divided by five. (IRS information on determining useful life and salvage value can be found in IRS Publication 534, *Tax Information on Depreciation.*) The method of depreciation used here is the simple "straight line method" which divides the cost by the number of years of useful life. There are other depreciation methods available such as the "double declining balance" and "some of the years digit" methods. To learn about them you should consult a basic accounting text.

You must take note that if you use your car for both business and personal purposes you can only deduct the portion of depreciation that is applicable to the percentage of your car's business use. For example, if you drove your car 10,000 miles and 2,000 was for business related purposes, you could deduct only 20% of the $1,300 depreciation or $260. On Schedule C–2, an example of this depreciation is filled out.

If you wish to avoid computing your gas, maintenance and depreciation expenses for tax purposes each year, you may deduct a standard mileage rate for each mile of your car's business use. For example, the 1979 rate was 17 cents a mile. Consult IRS Publication 17 for more information. Your best bet in any case is to compute your expenses both ways to see which yields the greatest tax deduction.

After you determine your net business income or loss, there are differences in the way it is taxed, depending on your type of organization. For a sole proprietorship, the net profit (loss) from Schedule C is entered on your Form 1040, U.S. Individual Income Tax Return as income from business. (Please see Figure 24.) Other types of income such as salaries from working and interest on savings would be added to this figure and you will be taxed on your total income. As a sole proprietor, you may also be liable for estimated tax payments and self-employment tax.

If your business is a partnership, no tax is paid by the partnership itself. The profit (loss) is divided among the partners according to the terms of the partnership agreement. Each partner is provided with an information schedule (Schedule K–1) from the partnership showing the amount to be reported as income on your regular personal income tax return (Form 1040).

Federal Self-Employment Tax

The purpose of the self-employment tax is to provide you with a social security coverage if you work for yourself. This tax is paid by a self-employed person in place of the social security tax withheld from an employee's wages. If you had income subject to self-employment tax, use Schedule SE to figure the tax. (See Figure 25). If you had more than one business, the profits and losses from all of your businesses should be combined on one Schedule SE. You must file Schedule SE if:

1. Your net earnings from self-employment was $400 or more, and
2. Your wages, from which social security tax was withheld, were less than $22,900 for 1979 (wage totals may differ for each year).

Estimated Tax

A sole proprietor or partner usually must file a declaration of estimated income tax on Form 1040ES (Figure 26). To determine if you are required to file for any year, you must first estimate your taxable income for that year. This will include your self-employment income and all other taxable income. You must also estimate how much of your income will be subject to withholding tax.

Form **1040**	Department of the Treasury—Internal Revenue Service **U.S. Individual Income Tax Return**	19**79**	

For Privacy Act Notice, see page 3 of Instructions | For the year January 1–December 31, 1979, or other tax year beginning , 1979, ending , 19

Use IRS label. Other-wise, please print or type.	Your first name and initial (if joint return, also give spouse's name and initial) **JOHN A.**	Last name **DOE**	Your social security number **012 : 34 : 5678**
	Present home address (Number and street, including apartment number, or rural route) **123 MAIN ST.**		Spouse's social security no.
	City, town or post office, State and ZIP code **ANYTOWN, CALIFORNIA 94305**	Your occupation ► **RETAILER** Spouse's occupation ►	

Presidential Election Campaign Fund ►
Do you want $1 to go to this fund? . . . . Yes ☐ No ☐
If joint return, does your spouse want $1 to go to this fund? . . . Yes ☐ No ☐
Note: Checking "Yes" will not increase your tax or reduce your refund.

Filing Status
Check only one box.

1 ☑ Single
2 ☐ Married filing joint return (even if only one had income)
3 ☐ Married filing separate return. Enter spouse's social security number above and full name here ► . . . .
4 ☐ Head of household. (See page 7 of Instructions.) If qualifying person is your unmarried child, enter child's name ► . . . .
5 ☐ Qualifying widow(er) with dependent child (Year spouse died ► 19). (See page 7 of Instructions.)

Exemptions

Always check the box labeled Yourself.
Check other boxes if they apply.

6a ☑ Yourself	☐ 65 or over	☐ Blind	Enter number of boxes checked on 6a and b ►
b ☐ Spouse	☐ 65 or over	☐ Blind	

c First names of your dependent children who lived with you ► - - - - - - - - - Enter number of children listed

d Other dependents: (1) Name	(2) Relationship	(3) Number of months lived in your home	(4) Did dependent have income of $1,000 or more?	(5) Did you provide more than one-half of dependent's support?	Enter number of other dependents ►

Add numbers entered in boxes above ► **1**

7 Total number of exemptions claimed . . . .

Income

Please attach Copy B of your Forms W–2 here.

If you do not have a W–2, see page 5 of Instructions.

8	Wages, salaries, tips, etc. *(LIST PART-TIME AND SUMMER JOBS)*	8	4,000	00
9	Interest income (attach Schedule B if over $400) *(FROM SAVINGS ACCOUNT)*	9	100	00
10a	Dividends (attach Schedule B if over $400) . . . . , 10b Exclusion			
c	Subtract line 10b from line 10a	10c		
11	State and local income tax refunds (does not apply unless refund is for year you itemized deductions—see page 10 of Instructions).	11		
12	Alimony received	12		
13	Business income or (loss) (attach Schedule C)	13	690	00
14	Capital gain or (loss) (attach Schedule D)	14		
15	Taxable part of capital gain distributions not reported on Schedule D (see page 10 of Instructions)	15		
16	Supplemental gains or (losses) (attach Form 4797)	16		
17	Fully taxable pensions and annuities not reported on Schedule E	17		
18	Pensions, annuities, rents, royalties, partnerships, estates or trusts, etc. (attach Schedule E)	18		
19	Farm income or (loss) (attach Schedule F)	19		
20a	Unemployment compensation. Total amount received			
b	Taxable part, if any, from worksheet on page 10 of Instructions	20b		
21	Other income (state nature and source—see page 10 of Instructions) ►	21		
22	**Total income.** Add amounts in column for lines 8 through 21 . . . . ►	22	4,790	00

Please attach check or money order here.

Adjustments to Income

23	Moving expense (attach Form 3903 or 3903F)	23				
24	Employee business expenses (attach Form 2106) . .	24				
25	Payments to an IRA (see page 11 of Instructions) . .	25				
26	Payments to a Keogh (H.R. 10) retirement plan . . .	26				
27	Interest penalty on early withdrawal of savings . . .	27				
28	Alimony paid (see page 11 of Instructions)	28				
29	Disability income exclusion (attach Form 2440) . . .	29				
30	Total adjustments. Add lines 23 through 29 . . . . ►			30		

Adjusted Gross Income

31	**Adjusted gross income.** Subtract line 30 from line 22. If this line is less than $10,000, see page 2 of Instructions. If you want IRS to figure your tax, see page 4 of Instructions . . . . ►	31	4,790	00

GOVERNMENT PRINTING OFFICE 1979 O-283-059 283-059-1 Form **1040** (1979)

Figure 24 – Form 1040 Individual Income Tax Return

Form 1040 (1980)   **Page 2**

Tax Computation
(See Instructions on page 11)

32	Amount from line 31 *(adjusted gross income)*	32	4,790 00
33	If you do not itemize deductions, enter zero . . . . }	33	0

If you itemize, complete Schedule A (Form 1040) and enter the amount from Schedule A, line 41 . . . }

Caution: If you have unearned income and can be claimed as a dependent on your parent's return, check here ▶ ☐ and see page 11 of the Instructions. Also see page 11 of the Instructions if:
- You are married filing a separate return and your spouse itemizes deductions, OR
- You file Form 4563, OR
- You are a dual-status alien.

34	Subtract line 33 from line 32. Use the amount on line 34 to find your tax from the Tax Tables, or to figure your tax on Schedule TC, Part I	34	4,790 00

Use Schedule TC, Part I, and the Tax Rate Schedules ONLY if:
- Line 34 is more than $20,000 ($40,000 if you checked Filing Status Box 2 or 5), OR
- You have more exemptions than are shown in the Tax Table for your filing status, OR
- You use Schedule G or Form 4726 to figure your tax.

Otherwise, you MUST use the Tax Tables to find your tax.

35	Tax. Enter tax here and check if from ☐ Tax Tables or ☐ Schedule TC	35	214 00
36	Additional taxes. (See page 12 of Instructions.) Enter here and check if from ☐ Form 4970, } ☐ Form 4972, ☐ Form 5544, ☐ Form 5405, or ☐ Section 72(m)(5) penalty tax . . . }	36	
37	**Total.** Add lines 35 and 36 . . . . ▶	37	214 00

Credits
(See Instructions on page 12)

38	Credit for contributions to candidates for public office . . .	38		
39	Credit for the elderly *(attach Schedules R&RP)*	39		
40	Credit for child and dependent care expenses (*attach Form 2441*) .	40		
41	Investment credit *(attach Form 3468)*	41		
42	Foreign tax credit *(attach Form 1116)*	42		
43	Work incentive (WIN) credit *(attach Form 4874)*	43		
44	Jobs credit *(attach Form 5884)*	44		
45	Residential energy credits *(attach Form 5695)*	45		
46	**Total credits.** Add lines 38 through 45		46	
47	**Balance.** Subtract line 46 from line 37 and enter difference (but not less than zero) . ▶		47	214 00

Other Taxes
(Including Advance EIC Payments)

48	Self-employment tax *(attach Schedule SE)*	48	55 89
49a	Minimum tax. Attach Form 4625 and check here ▶ ☐	49a	
49b	Alternative minimum tax. Attach Form 6251 and check here ▶ ☐	49b	
50	Tax from recomputing prior-year investment credit *(attach Form 4255)*	50	
51a	Social security (FICA) tax on tip income not reported to employer *(attach Form 4137)* . .	51a	
51b	Uncollected employee FICA and RRTA tax on tips *(from Form W–2)*	51b	
52	Tax on an IRA *(attach Form 5329)*	52	
53	Advance earned income credit (EIC) payments received *(from Form W–2)*	53	
54	**Balance.** Add lines 47 through 53 . . . . ▶	54	269 89

Payments
Attach Forms W–2, W–2G, and W–2P to front.

55	Total Federal income tax withheld	55	150 00	
56	1980 estimated tax payments and amount applied from 1979 return . .	56	100 00	
57	Earned income credit. If line 32 is under $10,000, see pages 13 and 14 of Instructions	57		
58	Amount paid with Form 4868	58		
59	Excess FICA and RRTA tax withheld (two or more employers)	59		
60	Credit for Federal tax on special fuels and oils *(attach Form 4136 or 4136–T)*	60		
61	Regulated Investment Company credit *(attach Form 2439)*	61		
62	**Total.** Add lines 55 through 61 . . . . ▶		62	250 00

Refund or Balance Due

63	If line 62 is larger than line 54, enter amount **OVERPAID** . . . . ▶	63	
64	Amount of line 63 to be **REFUNDED TO YOU** . . . . ▶	64	
65	Amount of line 63 to be applied to your 1981 estimated tax . . . ▶ 65		
66	If line 54 is larger than line 62, enter **BALANCE DUE.** Attach check or money order for full amount payable to "Internal Revenue Service." Write your social security number on check or money order . . ▶ (Check ▶ ☐ if Form 2210 (2210F) is attached. See page 15 of Instructions.) ▶ $	66	19 89

Please Sign Here

Under penalties of perjury, I declare that I have examined this return, including accompanying schedules and statements, and to the best of my knowledge and belief, it is true, correct, and complete. Declaration of preparer (other than taxpayer) is based on all information of which preparer has any knowledge.

▶ *John A. Doe*   4-15-80 ▶
Your signature   Date   Spouse's signature (if filing jointly, BOTH must sign even if only one had income)

Paid Preparer's Use Only

Preparer's signature and date ▶	Check if self-employed ▶ ☐	Preparer's social security no.
Firm's name (or yours, if self-employed) and address ▶	E.I. No. ▶	
	ZIP code ▶	

Figure 24 – Continued

SCHEDULE SE (Form 1040) Department of the Treasury Internal Revenue Service	**Computation of Social Security Self-Employment Tax** ▶ See Instructions for Schedule SE (Form 1040). ▶ Attach to Form 1040.	**1979** **14**

Name of self-employed person (as shown on social security card) JOHN A. DOE	Social security number of self-employed person ▶	012 : 34 : 5678

Part I Computation of Net Earnings from FARM Self-employment

Regular Method

1 Net profit or (loss) from:			
a Schedule F (Form 1040)	1a		
b Farm partnerships	1b		
2 Net earnings from farm self-employment (add lines 1a and 1b)	2		

Farm Optional Method

3 If gross profits from farming are:			
a Not more than $2,400, enter two-thirds of the gross profits . . . . }	3		
b More than $2,400 and the net farm profit is less than $1,600, enter $1,600 . . . . }			
4 Enter here and on line 12a, the amount on line 2, or line 3 if you elect the farm optional method .	4		

Part II Computation of Net Earnings from NONFARM Self-employment **SE**

Regular Method

5 Net profit or (loss) from:			
a Schedule C (Form 1040)	5a	690	00
b Partnerships, joint ventures, etc. (other than farming)	5b		
c Service as a minister, member of a religious order, or a Christian Science practitioner. (Include rental value of parsonage or rental allowance furnished.) If you filed Form 4361 and have not revoked that exemption, check here ▶ ☐ and enter zero on this line	5c		
d Service with a foreign government or international organization	5d		
e Other (specify) ▶..	5e		
6 Total (add lines 5a through 5e)	6	690	00
7 Enter adjustments if any (attach statement, see page 29 of Instructions)	7		
8 Adjusted net earnings or (loss) from nonfarm self-employment (line 6, as adjusted by line 7) . . .	8	690	00
Note: *If line 8 is $1,600 or more* **or** *if you do not elect to use the Nonfarm Optional Method, skip lines 9 through 11 and enter amount from line 8 on line 12b, Part III.*			

Nonfarm Optional Method

9 a Maximum amount reportable under both optional methods combined (**farm and nonfarm**) .	9a	$1,600	00
b Enter amount from line 3. (If you did not elect to use the farm optional method, enter zero.) . .	9b		
c Balance (subtract line 9b from line 9a)	9c		
10 Enter two-thirds of gross nonfarm profits or $1,600, whichever is smaller	10		
11 Enter here and on line 12b, the amount on line 9c or line 10, whichever is smaller	11		

Part III Computation of Social Security Self-employment Tax

12 Net earnings or (loss):			
a From farming (from line 4)	12a		
b From nonfarm (from line 8, or line 11 if you elect to use the Nonfarm Optional Method) . . .	12b	690	00
13 Total net earnings or (loss) from self-employment reported on lines 12a and 12b. (**If line 13 is less than $400, you are not subject to self-employment tax. Do not fill in rest of schedule**)	13	690	00
14 The largest amount of combined wages and self-employment earnings subject to social security or railroad retirement taxes for 1979 is	14	$22,900	00
15 a Total "FICA" wages (from Forms W-2) and "RRTA" compensation	15a			
b Unreported tips subject to FICA tax from Form 4137, line 9 or to RRTA	15b			
c Add lines 15a and 15b	15c	0	
16 Balance (subtract line 15c from line 14)	16	22,900	00
17 Self-employment income—line 13 or 16, whichever is smaller	17	690	00
18 Self-employment tax. (If line 17 is $22,900, enter $1,854.90; if less, multiply the amount on line 17 by .081.) Enter here and on Form 1040, line 48	18	55	89

☆ U.S. GOVERNMENT PRINTING OFFICE : 1979—O-283-068—95-1998423

Figure 25 – Schedule SE Social Security Self-Employment Tax

1979 Estimated Tax Worksheet (Keep for your records—Do Not Send to Internal Revenue Service)

1   Enter amount of Adjusted Gross Income you expect in 1980 . . . . _____

2 a   If you plan to itemize deductions, enter the estimated total of your deductions. If you
     do not plan to itemize deductions, skip to line 2c and enter zero . . . . _____

     $3,400 if married filing a joint return (or qualifying widow(er)) . . . .
    b Enter $2,300 if single (or head of household) . . . .
     $1,700 if married filing a separate return . . . .

    c   Subtract line 2b from line 2a (if zero or less, enter zero) . . . . _____

3   Subtract line 2c from line 1 . . . . _____

4   Exemptions (multiply $1,000 times number of personal exemptions) . . . . _____

5   Subtract line 4 from line 3 . . . . _____

6   **Tax.** (Figure tax on line 5 by using Tax Rate Schedule X, Y or Z in the 1979 Form 1040 instructions) . . _____

7   Enter any additional taxes from instruction B . . . . _____

8   Add lines 6 and 7 . . . . _____

9   Credits (credit for the elderly, credit for child care expenses, investment credit, residential energy credit, etc.) . _____

10   Subtract line 9 from line 8 . . . . _____

11   Tax from recomputing a prior year investment credit . . . . _____

12   Estimate of 1980 self-employment income $ ....; if $25,900 or more, enter $2,097.90,
     if less, multiply the amount by .081 (see instruction B for additional information) . . . . _____

13   Tax on premature distributions from an IRA . . . . _____

14   Add lines 10 through 13 . . . . _____

15   (a)   Earned income credit (see instruction B) . . . . _____
     (b)   Estimated income tax withheld and to be withheld during 1980 . . . . _____
     (c)   Credit for Federal tax on special fuels and oils (see Form 4136 or 4136-T) . . . _____
     (d)   Refundable business energy credit (see Schedule B (Form 3468)) . . . . . . _____

16   Total (add lines 15(a), (b), (c) and (d)) . . . . _____

17   Estimated tax (subtract line 16 from line 14). If $100 or more, fill out and file the declaration-voucher, if less,
     no declaration is required at this time . . . . _____

18   If the first declaration-voucher you are required to file is Number 1, due April 15, 1980, enter 1/4 of line 17
     here and on line 1 of your declaration-voucher(s) . . . . _____
     Note: *If you are not required to file Voucher No. 1 at this time, you may have to file by a later date. See
     instruction D(1).*

Page 2

Tear-off here

1040-ES Form Department of the Treasury Internal Revenue Service	**1979** Declaration- Voucher		
A. Estimated tax or amended estimated tax for the year ending **12 - 79** (month and year)	**B.** Overpayment from last year credited to estimated tax for this year		**Number 4**
	0		**(Calendar year—Due Jan. 15, 1980)**
$	$	Return this form with check or money order payable to the Internal Revenue Service.	
1 Amount from line 18 on worksheet . ▶	$ **100**		
2 Amount of any unused overpayment credit to be applied . . . . . ▶	**0**	Your social security number **012-34-5678**	Spouse's number, if joint declaration
3 Amount of this payment (subtract line 2 from line 1) . . . . . . ▶	$ **100**	First name and middle initial (of both spouses if joint declaration) **JOHN A.**	Last name **DOE**
If this is your first (or an amended) declaration for 1980, file even if line 3 is zero.		Address (Number and street) **123 MAIN ST**	
Sign here ▶ *John Doe* Your signature ▶ Spouse's signature (if joint declaration)		City, State, and ZIP code **ANYTOWN, CALIFORNIA 94305**	

283-072-1

Figure 26 – Form 1040-ES Federal Estimated Tax Worksheet

Your estimated tax is the amount by which the total of your estimated income tax and self-employment tax exceeds the expected withholding of tax from your pay. You need not file if your estimated tax can reasonably be expected to be less than $100. Part-time student businessmen and women should take note of this figure.

Form 1040ES (see Figure 26), has instructions, an estimated tax worksheet, and four declaration vouchers, (only one is shown here for illustration). Detach and mail a declaration voucher with each of your payments of estimated tax. Use the worksheet to figure your estimated tax and keep it in your records. You may pay your estimated tax in full with your declaration or in four equal installments on or before April 15, June 15, September 15, and January 15 of each year. The first payment must accompany a declaration. If at the end of the year you find a difference between your estimated tax paid in and your actual tax due for the end of that year (as already shown in Schedule C and Form 1065), then, when you file your personal income tax return at the end of the year, you will either pay in the difference or request a refund.

Tax Benefits — "Brilliant Deductions"

One of the greatest benefits of owning your own business is the tax advantage offered. Whereas employees have to pay a flat weekly rate from their payroll which does not allow for expenses, a business owner can take deductions for depreciation on a car if it is used for the business, telephone bills, travel expenses, newspaper and magazine subscriptions, and educational expenses which will lower the amount of reported net profit and hence the taxes that must be paid. Prospective student entrepreneurs should note that these deductions are allowed only if they can be related to the preparation, operation or enhancement of your business or personal business skills.

If you are an economics or business major, you can very well pay for most of your books and educational expenses out of your business (See Treasury Regulation 1, 162–5). For the last two quarters, I have been paying for most of my educational expenses and newspaper subscriptions (e.g., *The Wall Street Journal*) from my business revenues. One strategy available to a student entrepreneur is to pay himself a low salary out of the net profits and use the remainder to pay for business related-personal expenses. The IRS also offers tax credits for business investment in new manufacturing or energy conservation assets and for providing new jobs. Entrepreneurs may review IRS Publication 572 and 902 to see if they qualify.

For more information, call your local Internal Revenue Service office. Yes, they are in the phone book. Your tax dollars go to support the IRS and their taxpayer services, therefore you should take advantage of their "free" information and publications. I have both called and stopped by the local IRS office in San Jose and I have found them to be more than happy to help me out with questions and problems regarding my small business and tax requirements.

You should also make a point of attending the IRS Small Business Tax Workshops. These workshops are free and they do a very thorough job of going over all the business tax requirements and explaining step by step how to fill out the necessary forms. Even if you are debating on whether or not to establish your own business, I would still highly recommend your attending these workshops. They are tremendously informative regarding business in general, and a lot more practical than most of the classes that you would be taking in high school or college.

A list of IRS publications which you can use for reference is found below. Some of these I have already cited in my federal business tax descriptions.

Publication 17 Your Federal Income Tax

Publication 334 Tax Guide for Small Business

Publication 505 Tax Withholding and Declaration of Estimated Tax

Publication 533 Information on Self-Employment Tax

Publication 535 Tax Information on Business Equipment & Operating Losses

Publication 539 Withholding Taxes and Reporting Requirements

Publication 541 Tax Information on Partnership Income & Losses

Publication 542 Corporations and the Federal Income Tax

Publication 572 Investment Credit

Publication 589 Tax Information on Subchapter S Corporations

Publication 902 Targeted Jobs and Win Credits

Publication 1066 Small Business Tax Workbook

State Income and Self Employment Taxes

In the state of California, state income taxes must be filed if your total combined wages, interest, and part-time business income exceeds $5,000 for the year. Income requirements and regulations and tax rates may vary from state to state, and often do. Some states don't even have an income tax (believe it or not). Call your local state board of equalization or state department of taxation office for information on your state income tax laws.

In general, you will find your state income tax forms to be almost identical to your federal forms. Figure 27 is a sample of the California State Income tax form 540 which is quite similar to the federal form 1040. Figure 28 shows the California State Schedule C for computing net profit for a sole proprietorship which is modeled after the federal Schedule C. Likewise Figure 29 shows the California State Estimated Tax Worksheet and Declaration which is almost an exact replica of the federal form. All these forms are filled out in almost exactly the same manner as the federal forms so you should consult the previous sections for assistance in completing the forms.

If your state has a state income tax, you should stop by your local state income tax office or post office and pick up the state forms. Usually each state provides its own booklet explaining how to fill out the forms and the state tax rates on reported income.

Payroll Taxes

If you become an employer you will have to file federal and state payroll taxes. Here is where you will need your federal and state employment identification numbers which are discussed in section four, Figure 30 provides a chart which summarizes the type of federal and state payroll taxes that are required in Santa Clara County, California.

If you intend to become an employer you should contact the IRS to obtain a free Employers Tax Guide (IRS Publication #15). All your employees must fill out a Federal W-4 form, Employees Withholding Allowance Certificate, which you will use to determine their taxes from the payroll. The IRS requires employers to file a quarterly Payroll Tax Return (Form 941) and an Unemployment Tax Return (Form 940) if you pay wages of $1,500 or more in any calendar quarter. A W-2 form, Wage and Tax Statement, must be prepared for each one of your employees at year end. One copy of the W-2 form must be sent to the Social Security Administration with a W-3 form, Transmittal of Income and Tax Statements. Forms W-4, 941, 940, W-2 and W-3 are shown as Figures 31, 32, 33 and 34.

Most states also have income taxes on wages. You should contact your state department of employment for the requirements and forms of your state. Also, in addition to payroll taxes, many states require employers to have state unemployment and worker's compensation insurance. The chart on Figure 30 shows that in California the state requires payroll taxes on income for unemployment benefits, and for disability insurance (all filed on form DE 3 quarterly). Again, you should check the requirements of your state, because they may differ.

RESIDENT		TAXABLE
540		**1979**

CALIFORNIA
INDIVIDUAL INCOME TAX

YEAR

If you filed a Federal Form 1040A (short form) skip the items tinted green.

For Privacy Act Notice, see page 2 of Instructions | For the year January 1–December 31, 1979, or year ending_____, 1980.

Use Calif. label. Other-wise, please print or type.	Your first name and initial (if joint return, also give spouse's name and initial)	Last name	Your social security number
			Spouse's social security no.
	Present home address (Number and street, including apartment number, or rural route)		Your occupation
	City, town or post office, State and ZIP code		Spouse's occupation

Filing Status

Check only one box

1 ☐ Single
2 ☐ Married filing joint return (even if only one had income)
3 ☐ Married filing separate return. If spouse is also filing, give spouse's social security number in the space above and enter full name here_____
4 ☐ Head of household. Enter qualifying name _____. See page 4 of instructions.
5 ☐ Qualifying widow(er) with dependent child (Year spouse died 19____). See page 4 of instructions.

Exemption Credits

Always enter the credit for line 6a. Enter other credits if they apply.

6a Personal { If **box** checked on line 1 or 3, enter $27 { If **box** checked on line 2, 4 or 5, enter $54 ●		6a		00
6b Blind ☐ Yourself ☐ Spouse .... Number of boxes checked on 6b____ × $9		6b		00
6c Dependents—Do not list yourself, your spouse or the person who qualifies you as Head of household. Enter name and relationship. _____				
Total Number ■ ____ × $9 ●		6c		00
7 Total exemption credits claimed (Add lines 6a, 6b and 6c) Enter here and on line 38		7		00

Income

Please attach copy of your **Form(s) W-2 here.**

If you do not have a W-2, see page 4 of instructions.

Please attach **check** or **money** order here.

8 Wages, salaries, tips, etc. ●	8		
9 Interest income ....(attach Schedule B (540) if over $400) ●	9		
10 Dividends—before Federal exclusion ....(attach Schedule B (540) if over $400) ●	10		
11 State or Federal tax refunds are not taxable for State purposes			
12 Alimony received ●	12		
13 Business income or (loss).....................(attach Schedule C (540)) ●	13		
14 Capital gain or (loss).........................(attach Schedule D (540)) ●	14		
15 Gain on Sale of Principal Residence— If the once-in-a-lifetime exclusion is claimed—attach FTB 3535 and check box ☐			
16 Supplemental gains or losses ....(attach Schedule D-1 (540)) ●	16		
17 Fully taxable pensions and annuities not reported on Schedule E (540) ●	17		
18a Pensions and annuities .... } ●	18a		
18b Rents and royalties......... } ATTACH SCHEDULE E ●	18b		
18c Partnerships .... } (540) ●	18c		
18d Estates and trusts .... } ●	18d		
19 Farm income or (loss)........................(attach Schedule F (540)) ●	19		
20 Unemployment compensation is not taxable for State purposes			
21 Other income (state nature and source—see page 6 of instructions)_____ ●	21		
22 **Total income.** Add lines 8 through 21	22		

Adjustments to Income

23 Moving expense......................(attach FTB 3805U)...... ●	23			
24 Employee business expenses ....(attach FTB 3805N)...... ●	24			
25a Payments to an IRA..................(see page 7 of instructions)...... ●	25a			
25b Payments to a Keogh (H.R. 10) retirement plan ...... ●	25b			
25c Payments to a self-employed "Defined Benefit Plan"...... ●	25c			
26 Military exclusion..................(see page 7 of instructions)...... ●	26			
27 Interest penalty due to early withdrawal of savings.............. ●	27			
28 Alimony paid ....(see page 7 of instructions)...... ●	28			
(Paid to) _____ (Social Security Number) _____				
29 Disability income exclusion ....(attach FTB 3805T)...... ●	29			
30 **Total adjustments.** Add lines 23 through 29			30	

Adjusted Gross Income

31 **Adjusted gross income.** Subtract line 30 from line 22 (or enter line 22 if lines 23 through 30 not filled in) and continue on page 2 ■	31	

13

Page

Figure 27 – Form 540 California Income Tax Return

Form 540 (1979)

Tax Computation	**32** Amount from line 31. ... **32**

If you itemize deductions, enter sub-totals below:

a. Medical and dental expenses ... ● a.
b. Taxes ... ● b.
c. Interest expenses ... ● c.
d. Contributions ... ● d. [ATTACH SCHEDULE A (540)]
e. Casualty loss ... ● e.
f. Miscellaneous deductions ... ● f.
g. Net adoption expenses ... ● g.

33 Enter larger of **total itemized** or **standard deduction** ($1,100 if box checked on line 1 or 3 / $2,200 if box checked on line 2, 4 or 5) ... ● **33**
34 Taxable income. Subtract line 33 from line 32 ... ● **34**
35 Tax. Use the amount on line 34 to find your tax from ☐ Tax Table or ☐ Schedule G or G-1 (540) ... ● **35**
36 & 37 For tax on accumulation distribution of trusts get FTB 5870A

Credits
38 Enter amount from line 7. ... **38**
39 Credit for the elderly ... (attach Schedules R/RP (540)) ... ◉ **39**
40 Credit for child and dependent care expenses ... (attach FTB 3805X) ... ◉ **40**
41 **Special low income credit** ... (see page 9 of instructions) ... ■ **41**
42 "Other State" net income tax credit ... (attach Schedule S (540)) ... ◉ **42**
43 Agricultural irrigation equipment tax credit ... ◉ **43**
44 Jobs tax credits ... (attach FTB 3524) ... ◉ **44**
45 Solar energy credit ... (attach FTB 3805L) ... ◉ **45**
46 **Total credits.** Add lines 38 through 45 ... **46**
47 **Balance.** Subtract line 46 from line 35 and enter difference **(but not less than zero)** ... **47**

Other Taxes
48 Minimum tax on preference income ... (attach Schedule P (540)) ... ◉ **48**
49a Tax on an IRA ... (attach FTB 3805P) ... **49a**
49b Tax on a Keogh (HR 10) ... (attach statement with computations) ... **49b**
49 Total tax on IRA or Keogh. Add lines 49a and 49b ... ◉ **49**
50 Total tax liability. Add lines 47, 48 and 49 ... ■ **50**

Payments
Attach Form(s) W-2 and W-2P to front.
51 **Total California income tax withheld** ... ■ **51**
52 1979 California estimated tax payments and credit from 1978 return; and Filing extension payment ... ◆ **52**
53 Renter's credit—(attach Form 540RC (540)) (see page 10 of instructions) ... ■ **53**
54a Excess Calif. SDI tax withheld } [SEE PAGE 11 OF INSTRUCTIONS] ... ◆ **54a**
54b SDI Refund ... ■ **54b**
55 Total. Add lines 51 through 54b ... **55**

Refund
56 If line 55 is larger than line 50 enter amount **OVERPAID** ... ● **56**
57 Amount of line 56 to be **REFUNDED TO YOU** ... ■ **57**
Mail return to: Franchise Tax Board, P.O. Box 13-540, Sacramento, CA 95813
58 Amount of line 56 to be credited on **1980 estimated tax payment** ... ■ **58**

Balance Due
59 If line 50 is larger than line 55 enter **BALANCE DUE.** Attach check or money order for the full amount made payable to "Franchise Tax Board." Write your social security number on check or money order. ... ■ **59**
Mail return to: Franchise Tax Board, Sacramento, CA 95867
60 Check ► ☐ if Form 5805 (5805F) is attached. See page 11 of instructions. ► $_____

If you and your tax preparer do **not** need State income tax forms and instructions mailed to you next year, **see instructions, page 11, and check box.** ☐

Under penalties of perjury, I declare that I have examined this return, including accompanying schedules and statements, and to the best of my knowledge and belief, it is true, correct, and complete. Declaration of preparer (other than taxpayer) is based on all information of which preparer has any knowledge.

Your signature _____ Date _____ Spouse's signature (if filing jointly, BOTH must sign even if only one had income.)
Your Telephone Number (Optional) ( )

PLEASE SIGN HERE

Paid Preparer's Information
Preparer's signature ► _____
Firm's name (or yours, if self-employed), address and ZIP code ► _____ ► DATE

Do not write in this space
P
E
M
A
R

Reconciliation to Federal Return—If adjusted gross income on Federal Return is different from line 31, attach explanation.

78812-400 3-79 7,750M ① OSP

Figure 27 – Continued

SCHEDULE **C** FORM 540		**CALIFORNIA PROFIT (OR LOSS) FROM BUSINESS OR PROFESSION** (Sole Proprietorships) Partnerships, Joint Ventures, etc., Must File Form 565. ▶ Attach to Form 540 or 540NR ▶ See Instructions for Schedule C (Form 540).	TAXABLE **1979** YEAR

Name of proprietor	Social security number of proprietor

A Main business activity ▶ .... ; product ▶ ....

B Business name ▶ ....

C Employer identification number

D Business address (number and street) ▶ ....

City, State and ZIP code ▶ ....

E Accounting method: **(1)** ☐ Cash   **(2)** ☐ Accrual   **(3)** ☐ Other (specify) ▶ ....

F Method(s) used to value closing inventory:

(1) ☐ Cost   **(2)** ☐ Lower of cost or market   **(3)** ☐ Other (if other, attach explanation)

	Yes	No
G Was there any major change in determining quantities, costs, or valuations between opening and closing inventory? . . . If "Yes," attach explanation.		
H Did you deduct expenses for an office in your home? . . . . ▶		

PART I Income

1 a Gross receipts or sales	**1a**	
b Returns and allowances	**1b**	
c Balance (subtract line 1b from line 1a)	**1c**	
2 Cost of goods sold and/or operations (Schedule C-1, line 8)	**2**	
3 Gross profit (subtract line 2 from line 1c)	**3**	
4 Other income (attach schedule)	**4**	
5 Total income (add lines 3 and 4) . . . . ▶	**5**	

PART II Deductions

6 Advertising		**28** Telephone		
7 Amortization		**29** Travel and entertainment . . .		
8 Bad debts from sales or services .		**30** Utilities		
9 Bank charges		**31** Wages		
10 Car and truck expenses		**32** Other expenses (specify):		
11 Commissions		**a**		
12 Depletion		**b**		
13 Depreciation (explain in Schedule C-2)		**c**		
14 Dues and publications		**d**		
15 Employee benefit programs . .		**e**		
16 Freight (not included on Schedule C-1)		**f**		
17 Insurance		**g**		
18 Interest on business indebtedness .		**h**		
19 Laundry and cleaning		**i**		
20 Legal and professional services .		**j**		
21 Office supplies		**k**		
22 Pension and profit-sharing plans .		**l**		
23 Postage		**m**		
24 Rent on business property . . .		**n**		
25 Repairs		**o**		
26 Supplies (not included on Schedule C-1)		**p**		
27 Taxes		**q**		
		r		

33 Total deductions (add amounts in columns for lines 6 through 32r) . . . . ▶	**33**	
34 Net profit or (loss) (subtract line 33 from line 5). Enter here and on Form 540 or 540NR, line 13 ▶	**34**	

(Rev. 1979)   Page 1

Figure 28 – Schedule C California Profit (Loss) Statement

Schedule C (Form 540) 1979

SCHEDULE C-1.—Cost of Goods Sold and/or Operations

1 Inventory at beginning of year (if different from last year's closing inventory, attach explanation) . .	**1**	
2 **a** Purchases **2a**		
b Cost of items withdrawn for personal use **2b**		
c Balance (subtract line 2b from line 2a)	**2c**	
3 Cost of labor (do not include salary paid to yourself)	**3**	
4 Materials and supplies	**4**	
5 Other costs (attach schedule)	**5**	
6 Add lines 1, 2c, and 3 through 5	**6**	
7 Inventory at end of year	**7**	
8 Cost of goods sold and/or operations (subtract line 7 from line 6). Enter here and on Part I, line 2 ▶	**8**	

SCHEDULE C-2.—Depreciation   Note: Instructions for Guideline Class Life System and Class Life System are contained in the instructions for form FTB 3887 (Guideline Class Life System) and form FTB 3888 (Class Life System).

Description of property or group and guideline class (a)	Date acquired (b)	Cost or other basis (c)	Depreciation allowed or allowable in prior years (d)	Method of computing depreciation (e)	Life or rate (f)	Depreciation for this year (g)
1 Total additional first-year depreciation (do not include in items below)						
2 Depreciation from form FTB 3887 (See note above)						
3 Depreciation from form FTB 3888 (See note above)						
4 Other depreciation:						
Buildings						
Furniture and fixtures						
Transportation equipment						
Machinery and other equipment . .						
Other (specify)						
5 Totals				**5**		
6 Depreciation claimed in Schedule C-1				**6**		
7 Balance (subtract line 6 from line 5). Enter here and on Part II, line 13 . . . . ▶				**7**		

SCHEDULE C-3.—EXPENSE ACCOUNT INFORMATION

Enter information for yourself and your five highest paid employees. In determining the five highest paid employees, add expense account allowances to the salaries and wages. However, you don't have to provide the information for any employee for whom the combined amount is less than $25,000, or for yourself if your expense account allowance plus line 34, page 1; is less than $25,000.

Name (a)	Expense account (b)	Salaries and wages (c)
Owner		
1		
2		
3		
4		
5		

Did you claim a deduction for expenses connected with:	Yes	No
A Entertainment facility (boat, resort, ranch, etc.)?		
B Living accommodations (except employees on business)?		
C Employees' families at conventions or meetings?		
D Vacations for employees or their families not reported on Form W-2?		

Page 2

Figure 28 – Continued

1980 Estimated Tax Worksheet
(Keep for your records—Do not file)

1. Enter amount of Adjusted Gross Income you expect in 1980 1
2. **a** If you plan to **itemize deductions**, enter the estimated total of your deductions. If you do not plan to itemize deductions, skip this line 2a

   b Enter Standard Deduction { $1,100 if Single or Married filing separate . . . . $2,200 if Married filing joint, Head of household, or Qualifying widow(er) with dependent child . . . . } 2b

   c **Nonresident and part-year residents** (except active military) **must reduce the standard deduction:**

   California Adjusted Gross Income / Total Adjusted Gross Income = _____ % × line 2b 2c

   Enter the amount from the appropriate line 2a, 2b, or 2c. 2
3. Subtract line 2 from line 1 3
4. **Tax.** Find the tax on the amount on line 3 by using the Tax Table in Form 540 or 540NR instruction booklet 4
5. Exemption credits

   (a) Single or Married filing separate—$27. Married filing joint, Head of household or Qualifying widow(er) with dependent child—$54 . . . . 5a

   (b) Blind ☐ Yourself ☐ Your spouse—$9 for each box checked 5b

   (c) Dependents—$9 for each—Do not include yourself, your spouse or person who qualifies you as Head of household 5c

   (d) Add lines 5(a), 5(b) and 5(c) and (if applicable—multiply the total × _____% at line 2c) and enter the result on line 5 (Nonresident and part-year residents (except military) must reduce total exemption credits) 5d | 5
6. Subtract line 5 from line 4 6
7. Other credits (special low income tax credit, other state tax credit, renter's credit, etc.) 7
8. Subtract line 7 from line 6 8
9. Estimated California income tax withheld and to be withheld during 1980 9
10. Estimated tax (subtract line 9 from line 8). If $100 or more, fill out and file the declaration-voucher, if less, no declaration is required at this time. 10
11. If the first declaration-voucher you are required to file is: Number 1, due April 15, 1980, enter ¼ . . . . Number 2, due June 16, 1980, enter ⅓ . . . Number 3, due September 15, 1980, enter ½ . . Number 4, due January 15, 1981, enter amount . . } of line 10 here and on line 1 of your declaration-voucher(s) } (Please round off to whole dollars) . . . . | 11 | 00

MAIL YOUR DECLARATION-VOUCHER(S) TO "FRANCHISE TAX BOARD, 540ES BOX, SACRAMENTO, CA 95867"

------------------------------ CUT HERE ------------------------------

FORM 540ES   🏛 *CALIFORNIA*   Declaration of Estimated Income Tax   **YEAR 1980**

Declaration Voucher **4**
(Calendar year—Due Jan. 15, 1981)

A. Estimated tax or amended estimated tax for the year ending _____ (month and year)   **B.** Overpayment from last year credited to estimated tax for this year

Mail this voucher with check or money order payable to "**Franchise Tax Board**" 540ES Box, Sacramento, California 95867. To insure proper credit to your account please enter your social security number on your check or money order.

$ _____ .00 | $ _____ .00

1 Amount from line 11 on worksheet ► $ _____ .00
2 Amount of any unused overpayment credit to be applied . . . . ► _____ .00
3 Amount of this payment (subtract line 2 from line 1) . . . . ► $ _____ .00

If this is your first (or an amended) declaration for 1980, file even if line 3 is zero.

Your social security number | Spouse's number, if joint declaration

First name and middle initial (of both spouses if joint declaration) | Last name

Sign here ► Your signature

Spouse's signature (if joint declaration)

Address (Number and street)

City, State, and ZIP code

Please type or print

13   70831-400 10-79 1,904M OSP

Figure 29 – California Estimated Tax Worksheet

California Payroll Taxes—1981

Type of Tax	Employer Rate	Employee Rate	Form	Report Period
Income Tax				
Federal	0	Determined by exemptions	941	Quarterly
State	0	claimed on W-4[1]	DE3	Quarterly
FICA				
(Social Security)	6.35%	6.35%	941	Quarterly
Unemployment				
Federal (FUTA)	3.4%			
less state credit	−2.7%			
effective rate	.7%	0	940	Annually
State (SUI)	3.3%[2]	0	DE3	Quarterly
Disability (SDI)	.6%	0	DE3	Quarterly

1. Californians may claim exemptions on W-4 or on the state's form DE 4.

2. New employers will be taxed at this rate. Thereafter, the rate is revised annually.

Figure 30 – Payroll Chart

Form **W-4** (Rev. December 1978) Department of the Treasury Internal Revenue Service	**Employee's Withholding Allowance Certificate** (Use for Wages Paid After December 31, 1978) This certificate is for income tax withholding purposes only. It will remain in effect until you change it. If you claim exemption from withholding, you will have to file a new certificate on or before April 30 of next year.

Type or print your full name
EMPLOY   YEE

Your social security number
245-67-8940

Home address (number and street or rural route)
152 MANZANITA

City or town, State, and ZIP code
STANFORD, CA 94305

Marital Status
☑ Single　☐ Married
☐ Married, but withhold at higher Single rate
Note: *If married, but legally separated, or spouse is a nonresident alien, check the single block.*

1　Total number of allowances you are claiming *1*

2　Additional amount, if any, you want deducted from each pay (if your employer agrees) . . . . $ *0*

3　I claim exemption from withholding (see instructions). Enter "Exempt" . . . .

Under the penalties of perjury, I certify that the number of withholding allowances claimed on this certificate does not exceed the number to which I am entitled. If claiming exemption from withholding, I certify that I incurred no liability for Federal income tax for last year and I anticipate that I will incur no liability for Federal income tax for this year.

Signature ► *Employ Yee*　　　Date ► *4/15*　　　, 19 *79*

---------------------- Detach along this line ----------------------

▲　*Give the top part of this form to your employer; keep the lower part for your records and information*　▲

Instructions

The explanatory material below will help you determine your correct number of withholding allowances, and will assist you in completing the Form W-4 at the top of this page.

See **Publication 505** for more information on withholding.

Avoid Overwithholding or Underwithholding

By claiming the number of withholding allowances you are entitled to, you can fit the amount of tax withheld from your wages to your tax liability. In addition to the allowances for personal exemptions to be claimed in item (a), be sure to claim any additional allowances you are entitled to in item (b), "Special withholding allowance," and item (c), "Allowance(s) for credit(s) and/or deduction(s)." While you may claim these allowances on Form W-4 for withholding purposes, you may not claim them under "Exemptions" on your tax return Form 1040 or Form 1040A.

You may claim the special withholding allowance if you are single with only one employer, or married with only one employer and your spouse is not employed. If you have unusually large itemized deductions, make alimony payments, or credit(s) for child care expenses, earned income, credit for the elderly, or residential energy credits, you may claim additional allowances to avoid having too much income tax withheld from your wages.

If you and your spouse are both employed or you have more than one employer, you should make sure that enough has been withheld. If you find that you need more withholding, claim fewer allowances or ask for additional withholding or request to be withheld at the higher "Single" status. If you are currently claiming additional withholding allowances based on itemized deductions, check the worksheet on the back to see that you are claiming the proper number of allowances.

How Many Withholding Allowances May You Claim?

Use the schedule below to determine the number of allowances you may claim for tax withholding purposes. In determining the number, keep in mind these points: if you are single and hold more than one job, you may not claim the same allowances with more than one employer at the same time; or, if you are married and both you and your spouse are employed, you may not both claim the same allowances with your employers at the same time. A nonresident alien, other than a resident of Canada, Mexico, or Puerto Rico, may claim only one personal allowance.

Completing Form W-4

If you find you are entitled to one or more allowances in addition to those you are now claiming, increase your number of allowances by completing the form above and filing it with your employer. If the number of allowances you previously claimed decreases, you must file a new Form W-4 within 10 days. (If you expect to owe more tax than will be withheld, you may increase your withholding by claiming fewer or "0" allowances on line 1, or by asking for additional withholding on line 2, or both.)

You may claim exemption from withholding of Federal income tax if you had no liability for income tax for last year, and you anticipate that you will incur no liability for income tax for this year. You may not claim exemption if your joint or separate return shows tax liability before the allowance of any credit for income tax withheld. If you are exempt, your employer will not withhold Federal income tax from your wages. However, social security tax will be withheld if you are covered by the Federal Insurance Contributions Act.

You must revoke this exemption (1) within 10 days from the time you anticipate you will incur income tax liability for the year or (2) on or before December 1 if you anticipate you will incur Federal income tax liability for the next year. If you want to stop or are required to revoke this exemption, you must file a new Form W-4 with your employer showing the number of withholding allowances you are entitled to claim. This certificate for exemption from withholding will expire on April 30 of next year unless a new Form W-4 is filed on or before that date.

The Following Information is Provided in Accordance with the Privacy Act of 1974

The Internal Revenue Code requires every employee to furnish his or her employer with a signed withholding certificate showing the number of withholding allowances that the employee claims (section 3402(f)(2)(A) and the Regulations thereto). Individuals are required to provide their Social Security Number for proper identification and processing (section 6109 and the Regulations thereto).

The principal purpose for soliciting withholding allowance certificate information is to administer the Internal Revenue laws of the United States.

If an employee does not furnish a signed withholding allowance certificate, the employee is considered as claiming no withholding allowances (section 3401(e)) and shall be treated as a single person (section 3402(l)).

The routine uses of the withholding allowance certificate information include disclosure to the Department of Justice for actual or potential criminal prosecution or civil litigation.

Figure Your Total Withholding Allowances Below

(a)　Allowance(s) for exemption(s)—Enter 1 for each personal exemption you can claim on your Federal income tax return* . . .　*1*

(b)　Special withholding allowance—Enter 1 if single with 1 employer, or married with 1 employer and spouse not employed** . . .

(c)　Allowance(s) for credit(s) and/or deduction(s)—Enter number from tables on **page 2** . . . .

(d)　Total (add lines (a) through (c) above)—Enter here and on line 1, Form W-4, above . . . .　*1*

*If you are in doubt as to whom you may claim as a dependent, see the instructions that came with your last Federal income tax return or call your local Internal Revenue Service office.
**This allowance is used solely for purposes of figuring your withholding tax, and cannot be claimed when you file your tax return.

263-037-1

Figure 31 – W-4 Employee's Withholding Allowance Certificate

Form **941**
(Rev. April 1980)
Department of the Treasury
Internal Revenue Service

Employer's Quarterly Federal Tax Return

Your name, address, employer identification number, and calendar quarter of return. (If not correct, please change)

Name (as distinguished from trade name)   Date quarter ended

Trade name, if any   Employer identification number

Address and ZIP code

	T	
	FF	
	FD	
	FP	
	I	
	T	

If address is different from prior return, check here ▶

1 Number of employees (except household) employed in the pay period that includes March 12th (complete for first quarter only)
2 Total wages and tips subject to withholding, plus other compensation ⟶
3 Total income tax withheld from wages, tips, annuities, gambling, etc.
4 Adjustment of withheld income tax for preceding quarters of calendar year
5 Adjusted total of income tax withheld ⟶
6 Taxable FICA wages paid . . . . . . $............ multiplied by 12.26% = TAX
7 Taxable tips reported . . . . . . $............ multiplied by 6.13% = TAX
8 Total FICA taxes (add lines 6 and 7)
9 Adjustment of FICA taxes (see instructions)
10 Adjusted total of FICA taxes ⟶
11 Total taxes (add lines 5 and 10)
12 Advance earned income credit (EIC) payments, if any (see instructions)
13 Net taxes (subtract line 12 from line 11)

Record of Federal Tax Deposits (See instructions on page 4)

Deposit period ending:	I. Tax liability for period	II. Date of deposit	III. Amount deposited
Overpayment from previous quarter. . . .			
First month of quarter — 1st through 7th day			
8th through 15th day			
16th through 22d day			
23d through last day			
A First month total [A]			
Second month of quarter — 1st through 7th day			
8th through 15th day			
16th through 22d day			
23d through last day			
B Second month total [B]			
Third month of quarter — 1st through 7th day			
8th through 15th day			
16th through 22d day			
23d through last day			
C Third month total [C]			
D Total for quarter (add items A, B, and C) .			
E Final deposit made for quarter. (Enter zero if the final deposit made for the quarter is included in item D) .			

14 Total deposits for quarter (including final deposit made for quarter) and overpayment from previous quarter. (See instructions for deposit requirements on page 4.)
Note: If undeposited taxes at the end of the quarter are $200 or more, deposit the full amount with an authorized financial institution or a Federal Reserve bank according to the instructions on the back of the Federal Tax Deposit Form 501. Enter this deposit in the Record of Federal Tax Deposits and include it on line 14.
15 Undeposited taxes due (subtract line 14 from line 13—this should be less than $200). Pay to Internal Revenue Service and enter here ⟶
16 If line 14 is more than line 13, enter overpayment here ▶ $ and check if to be: ☐ Applied to next return, or ☐ Refunded.
17 Number of Forms W-4 enclosed. Do not send originals. (See General and Specific Instructions.)
18 If you are not liable for returns in the future, write "FINAL" (see instructions) ▶   Date final wages paid ▶

Under penalties of perjury, I declare that I have examined this return, including accompanying schedules and statements, and to the best of my knowledge and belief it is true, correct, and complete.

Date ▶   Signature ▶   Title ▶

Please file this form with your internal Revenue Service Center (see instructions on "Where to File").   Form **941** (Rev. 4-80)

Figure 32 – Form 941 Employers Quarterly Federal Tax Return

Form **940** Department of the Treasury Internal Revenue Service	**Employer's Annual Federal Unemployment Tax Return**	**1980**

If incorrect, make any necessary ▶ change	Name (as distinguished from trade name) Trade name, if any Address and ZIP code	Calendar Year **1979** Employer identification number

T	
FF	
FD	
FP	
I	
T	

A Have you paid all required contributions to your State unemployment fund by the due date of Form 940? . . . . . . ☐ Yes ☐ No

If you check the "Yes" box, enter amount of contributions timely paid to your State unemployment fund . . . ▶..............

B Are you required to pay contributions to only one State? . . . . ☐ Yes ☐ No

If you check the "Yes" box: (1) Enter the name of the State that you are required to pay contributions to . . ▶..............

(2) Enter your State experience rate(s) for 1979 (see instructions for Part V, columns 4 and 5) . ▶ _____%, _____%, _____%

Part I   **Computation of Taxable Wages (To Be Completed by All Taxpayers)**

1 Total payments (including exempt payments) during the calendar year for services of employees . . . . .

Exempt Payments	**Amount paid**
2 Exempt payments. (Explain each exemption shown, attaching additional sheets if necessary) ▶	
3 Payments for services in excess of $6,000. Enter only the excess over the first $6,000 paid to individual employees exclusive of exempt amounts entered on line 2. Do not use State wage limitation . .	

4 Total exempt payments (add lines 2 and 3) . . . .

5 Total taxable wages (subtract line 4 from line 1). (If any portion is exempt from State contributions, see instructions) . . ▶

Part II   **Tax Due or Refund (Complete if You Checked the "Yes" boxes in Both Items A and B Above)**

1 FUTA tax. Multiply the wages on line 5, Part I, by .007 and enter here . . . .

2 (a) Delaware wages included on line 5, Part I . . ▶ $.................... multiplied by .003 . . .

   (b) Pennsylvania wages included on line 5, Part I . ▶ $.................... multiplied by .003 . . .

3 Total FUTA tax (add lines 1, 2a, and 2b) . . . .

4 Less: Total FUTA tax deposited from line 5, Part IV . . . .

5 Balance due (subtract line 4 from line 3—this should not be over $100). Pay to Internal Revenue Service . . ▶

6 Overpayment (subtract line 3 from line 4) . . . . ▶

Part III   **Tax Due or Refund (Complete if You Checked the "No" Box in Either Item A or Item B Above)**

1 Gross FUTA tax. Multiply the wages on line 5, Part I, by .034 . . . .

2 Maximum credit. Multiply the wages on line 5, Part I, by .027 . . . .

3 Enter the smaller of the amount on line 11, Part V, or line 2, above . . . .

4 (a) Delaware wages included on line 5, Part I . ▶ $.................... multiplied by .003

   (b) Pennsylvania wages included on line 5, Part I . ▶ $.................... multiplied by .003

5 Credit allowable (subtract lines 4a and 4b from line 3) . . . .

6 Net FUTA tax (subtract line 5 from line 1) . . . .

7 Less: Total FUTA tax deposited from line 5, Part IV . . . .

8 Balance due (subtract line 7 from line 6—this should not be over $100). Pay to Internal Revenue Service . . ▶

9 Overpayment (subtract line 6 from line 7) . . . . ▶

Part IV   **Record of Federal Tax Deposits for Unemployment Tax (Form 508)**

	a. Quarter	b. Liability by period	c. Date of deposit	d. Amount of deposit
1	First			
2	Second			
3	Third			
4	Fourth			

5 Total FUTA tax deposited (add column d, lines 1 through 4) (do not include contributions paid to State) . . ▶

If you will not have to file returns in the future, write "Final" here (see general instruction "Who Must File") . . ▶

Under penalties of perjury, I declare that I have examined this return, including accompanying schedules and statements, and to the best of my knowledge and belief, it is true, correct, and complete, and that no part of any payment made to a State unemployment fund claimed as a credit was or is to be deducted from the payments to employees.

Date ▶   Signature ▶   Title (Owner, etc.) ▶

283-044-2   Form **940** (1979)

Figure 33 – Form 940 Employers Annual Federal Unemployment Tax Return

1 Control number	22222		

2 Employer's name, address, and ZIP code		3 Employer's identification number	4 Employer's State number

	5 Stat. employee / Deceased / Pension plan / Legal rep.	942 emp. / Sub-total / Correction / Void
	6	7 Advance EIC payment

8 Employee's social security number	9 Federal income tax withheld	10 Wages, tips, other compensation	11 FICA tax withheld
12 Employee's name, address, and ZIP code		13 FICA wages	14 FICA tips
		16 Employer's use	
		17 State income tax	18 State wages, tips, etc.	19 Name of State
		20 Local income tax	21 Local wages, tips, etc.	22 Name of locality

Form **W-2 Wage and Tax Statement** 1980   Copy B To be filed with employee's FEDERAL tax return. This information is being furnished to the Internal Revenue Service.   Department of the Treasury Internal Revenue Service

Instructions for Preparing Form W–2

The 6-part wage and tax statement is acceptable in most States. If you are in doubt, ask your appropriate State or local official.

Prepare Form W–2 for each of your employees to whom any of the following items applied during 1980.

(a) You withheld income tax or FICA (social security) tax.

(b) You would have withheld income tax if the employee had not claimed more than one withholding allowance.

(c) You paid $600 or more.

(d) You paid for services any amount, if you are in a trade or business. Include the cash value of any payment you made that was not in cash.

By January 31, 1981, give Copies B, C, and 2 to each person who was your employee during 1980. For anyone who stopped working for you before the end of 1980, you may give copies any time after employment ends. If the employee asks for Form W–2, give him or her the completed copies within 30 days of the request or the final wage payment, whichever is later. Send Copy A to the Social Security Administration by February 28, 1981. (For more information, please see Forms 941, 942, W–3, or Circular E. Farmers, see Circular A.)

See separate **Instructions for Forms W–2 and W–2P** for more information on how to complete Form W–2.

☆ U.S. GOVERNMENT PRINTING OFFICE : 1980—283-030 EI-36-2441915

Figure 34 – W-2 and W-3 Wage and Tax Statements

A possible alternative to the employer's payroll and insurance tax burden is to hire people as "independent contractors" rather than as employees. This way, you don't have to keep separate payroll tax records for each employee which causes a whole mess of paperwork. By hiring people as independent contractors you will only have to file an annual Federal 1099 form, Statement of Miscellaneous Earnings, along with form 1096, Annual Summary and Transmittal of U.S. Information Returns, and independent contractors must take care of their own taxes on their personal tax return. This will save you a lot of time and money in terms of cutting down on added paperwork and payroll tax hassles. Consult your local IRS, and perhaps your accountant (now may be the time for you to hire one), to see if you can hire out your work on an independent contracting basis.

Entrepreneurial Studies

In one of my conversations with Brett Johnson, we discussed our mutual concern that there is so little practical business training at most of the nation's major liberal arts colleges and universities. For instance, the schools we attend, Harvard and Stanford, have no organizations or departments geared toward assisting or training student entrepreneurs and very few courses on the subject. Generally speaking, if you are going to go into business on your own, you are literally going to have to do it by yourself.

There are exceptions to the rule, however. Many schools offer one or more courses in entrepreneurial studies and several of these schools have fully-developed programs in venture management.[1] If becoming an entrepreneur is your primary goal, you might consider enrolling in one of these programs. Many successful entrepreneurs have launched their businesses as a direct result of participation in such courses of study.

Professor Karl H. Vesper, a professor at the University of Washington has compiled a list of collegiate entrepreneurial courses and endowed chairs in a book entitled *Entrepreneurship Education* published by the Babson College Center for Entrepreneurial Studies. Professor Vesper, who has a Masters Degree in Business Administration from Harvard and a Masters Degree in mechanical engineering from Stanford, says that in 1969 when he first started compiling information on entrepreneurial courses already in operation, only 16 schools offered courses. Now there are seven endowed chairs and hundreds of courses offered in entrepreneurial management, financing, marketing, and accounting at 98 colleges and universities around the country.[2]

---

[1]Venture Magazine, December 1979, pp. 67–72 "How Business Schools Handle Entrepreneurs." by Susan Schoch.

[2]Nations Business, September 1980, "Want To Be An Entrepreneur? Go to College," by Robert Graham.

You may obtain a copy of Professor Vesper's book by writing to:

Babson Center for Entrepreneurial Studies
Babson College
Wellesley, Massachusetts 02157

The book has 300 pages and its price is $10.

Professor Vesper is also the author of the book, *New Venture Strategies* (Prentice-Hall 1980) which I have cited in the reading list as recommended reading.

For those college entrepreneurs who are considering attending Graduate School of Business Programs the chart on "Graduate Courses for Entrepreneurs" compiled by *Venture Magazine* may prove to be helpful in making their decision. The chart is shown on Figure 35.

University of Southern California

The University of Southern California has a one-year entrepreneurial program which combines theory with practice. In the fall semester, the students study concepts that are basic to the establishment of a new enterprise. In the second semester, the students must formulate and present a detailed plan for a proposed business venture. While they are not required to put the plan into action, many students have done so; others have implemented their proposals soon after graduating from the program. The program is under the direction of Dr. Rick Buskirk, and can be taken at either the undergraduate or graduate level.

Discovery Properties

Bruce Birkeland went into the first year class of USC's entrepreneurial program in 1971. While he was enrolled in the program Birkeland worked part-time for the Newport Equities Trust, a real estate development firm in Newport Beach. The entrepreneurial program really turned Birkeland on to starting his own real estate company. Upon graduation, Bruce started his own real estate venture called Discovery Properties with a fellow graduate from the USC Master of Science Program in Entrepreneurship and Venture Management.

During the first year their venture got off to a slow start and Birkeland's partner decided to bail out. But Birkeland's tenacity made him stick with his new venture and make it a success. In addition to owning and leasing its own properties, the firm currently handles brokerage, investment sales and provides a property management service. The firm's pro-

Graduate Courses For Entrepreneurs

The following schools offer either a program of concentration or one or more course in new ventures on the graduate level only. These schools and others also may offer undergraduate programs and electives. The methods of instruction are indicated.

School	Program or	# of Electives	# of Lecturers	Case Studies	Course Work Projects	Visits by Entrepreneurs
Babson College, Babson Park, MA	–	2	4	x	x	x
Baltimore, Univ. of; Baltimore, MD	–	10	10	x	–	x
Baylor Univ., Waco, TX	–	1	3	x	–	x
Boston College, Chestnut Hill, MA	–	3	3	x	x	–
Calgary, Univ. of; Alberta, CAN	–	4	5	x	x	–
California, Univ. of; Berkeley, CA	–	1	2	–	x	–
California, Univ. of; Los Angeles, CA	–	3	2	x	–	x
California, Univ. of; Riverside, CA	–	1	1	x	x	x
Carnegie-Mellon Univ., Pittsburgh, PA	–	1	2	x	x	x
Chicago, Univ. of; Chicago, IL	–	1	2	x	x	x
Cincinnati, Univ. of; Cincinnati, OH	–	1	1	x	–	x
Cleveland State Univ., Cleveland, OH	–	2	1	x	x	–
Columbia University; New York, NY	–	2	1	x	x	x
Connecticut, Univ. of; Storrs, CT	–	1	3	x	x	x
Cornell Univ., Ithaca, NY	–	1	1	x	–	–
Dartmouth College, Hanover, NH	–	2	2	x	x	x
Duke Univ., Durham, NC	–	2	1	x	x	x
Fordham Univ., Bronx, NY	–	1	1	x	–	x
Georgia State Univ., Atlanta, GA	–	2-3	4-5	x	x	x
Grand Valley State College, Allendale, MH	–	1	1	–	x	x
Harvard Univ., Boston, MA	x	–	7	x	–	–
Hawaii, Univ. of; Honolulu, HI	–	1	1	x	x	x
Illinois, Univ. of; Urbana, IL	–	1	1	x	–	–
Indiana, Univ. of; Bloomington, IN	x	–	20	x	x	–
Iowa, Univ. of; Iowa City, IA	–	1	1	x	–	x
Maine, Univ. of; Portland, ME	–	1	1	x	x	x
Michigan, Univ. of; Ann Arbor, MH	–	3	3	x	x	x
MIT, Cambridge, MA	–	2	2	x	–	x
New Hampshire, Univ. of; Durham, NH	–	2-3	5	x	x	x
New York Univ., New York, NY	–	1	2	x	x	x
North Carolina, Univ. of; Chapel Hill, NC	–	2-3	1	x	x	x
Northeastern Univ., Boston, MA	–	3	12	x	x	x
Northwestern Univ., Evanston, IL	–	1	–	x	x	x
Ohio State Univ., Columbus, OH	–	3	3	x	–	x
Oklahoma State Univ., Stillwater, OK	–	1	1	x	–	x
Oklahoma, Univ. of; Norman, OK	x	–	5	x	x	x
Rhode Island, Univ. of; Kingston, RI	–	1	1	–	x	–
Rochester, Univ. of; Rochester, NY	–	1	2	x	–	x
Rutgers State Univ., Camden NJ	–	1	1	x	x	x
San Diego State Univ., San Diego, CA	–	2	1	x	x	x
Southern California, Univ. of; Los Angeles, CA	x	–	4	x	x	x
Southern Methodist Univ., Dallas, TX	x	–	2	–	x	x
St. Louis Univ., St. Louis, MO	–	1	1	x	x	x
Temple Univ., Philadelphia, PA	x	–	4	x	x	x
Tennessee, Univ., of; Knoxville, TN	–	1	5-6	x	x	x
Texas Technical Univ., Lubbock, TX	–	2	3	x	–	–
Tulane Univ., New Orleans, LA	–	1	1	–	x	–
Valdosta State College, Valdosta, GA	–	1-2	1	–	x	–
Washington, Univ. of; Seattle, WA	–	3	3	x	x	x
Wharton School, University Park, PA	x	–	6	x	x	x
Wichita State Univ., Wichita, KA	x	–	3	x	x	x
Stanford Univ., Stanford, CA	–	1	3	x	x	x
Wisconsin, Univ., of; Milwaukee, WI	–	1	1	x	x	–
Wright State Univ., Dayton, OH	–	1	1	–	x	x
Xavier Univ., Cincinnati, OH	–	1	2	x	x	–

Schools will offer either a program of study (indicated by an "x") or individual courses (the number of courses is indicated). Schools employ three methods of teaching: case studies, student projects, and lectures from entrepreneurs. Individual methods of each school are indicated by an "x" under the appropriate column.

Compiled by Joan Delaney

Figure 35 – Graduate Courses for Entrepreneurs

perty management service has a portfolio of industrial parks, shopping centers, and office buildings totaling nearly 3,000,000 square feet.

Brandon House Designs

Brendon Baker is another successful product of USC's entrepreneurial program. He submitted a venture proposal for a business dealing in silk-screened wall-hangings, a business which he started while he was enrolled in the program back in 1973, and continues to run today. The business idea itself was an outgrowth of his attempts to decorate his apartment. Unable to afford expensive paintings or lithographs, he tried using decorator fabrics stretched across picture frames. He and his partner were so pleased with the results that they decided to make a business out of it. They hired designers and contracted the silk-screening out to local shops, and sold the finished product to retail outlets of various kinds. What started out as a venture proposal is now a flourishing business called Brendon House Designs, which generated more than $1 million in volume in 1980.

Baylor University

Baylor University's Center for Private Enterprise and Entrepreneurship in Waco, Texas has attracted national attention in articles in newspapers and magazines across the country. The Center was founded about a year and a half ago by Dr. Calvin Kent, who currently serves as director of the program. The Center offers a Bachelors of Business Administration (BBA) in Entrepreneurship and Venture Management. The center not only teaches students the basics needed for new enterprise management but also encourages students to start their own companies. The "Venture Assistance Program" helps students develop business plans, market feasibility studies, and pro-forma financial statements for new venture ideas. Brent Pennington, the Safe-T-Stat inventor, was enrolled in this program.

Baylor also has a special program aimed at educating elementary and high school-age students. Under this program, which is run by Professor John Pischiotta, Baylor professors give classes on private enterprise and economics. The program is funded by local businesses. Professors and businessmen alike see this program as very beneficial because it gives the students early exposure to the fundamentals of the American free enterprise system. It is felt that entrepreneurs are developed long before they attend college, and that the entrepreneurial spirit is something that cannot be taught. This spirit has to be ignited while the student is very young, and developed by providing an encouraging environment.

Carnegie-Mellon University

Professor Dwight Bauman founded the Center for Entrepreneurial Development Program at Carnegie-Mellon in 1971, after fifteen years of teaching at MIT, because he believed that neither engineering nor business schools were doing an adequate job of developing entrepreneurs. The Center for Entrepreneurial Development not only trains and assists students in developing their business plans but it also has a non-profit revolving fund which is used to finance the start-up costs of the student's new business proposals. In 1973, the Center received a $1 million grant from the National Science Foundation to develop the program. Since 1978, the Center has been operating on donations from enterprises which the program and the revolving fund helped initiate.

Most of the students who start their own companies through the Center are either current or former graduate students in the business or engineering departments although the program is open to the entire Carnegie-Mellon community. So far the Center has proven to be very successful. It is responsible for assisting in the establishing and management of over a dozen new businesses. Elcomp Systems is one of them.

Elcomp Systems, Inc.

Ami Ellis came to the United States from Israel in 1976 in order to obtain his Masters Degree in Business Administration from Carnegie-Mellon University. In the beginning of his second year in the MBA program, Ellis began a classroom project in a class called "Design and Entrepreneurship" which has blossomed into a million dollar business called Elcomp Systems, Inc. Elcomp designs computer programs which process all paper work, medical records, insurance reports, and accounting for medical offices. It handles the purchasing and installation of the computer and specifically designs a program to meet its client's needs. Elcomp also trains the office workers to use the program and handles follow-up training and maintenance requirements. In 1980, Elcomp did $1 million in gross sales and expects to do more than twice that amount this year.

Among other schools with special programs are: Cornell University which recently received a one million dollar grant from former student Donald Berens to set up small business and entrepreneurial courses; Southern Methodist University which offers entrepreneurial courses through the Caruth Institute of Owner Managed Business; and, of course, there is Babson College whose program has inspired so many students to go into business that it actually has its own Chamber of Commerce.

Entrepreneurial Studies

SCIRE PROJECT APPLICATION

Note: Please read the SCIRE credit approval guidelines on the back of this form
before writing your proposal. Proposals in their final form are due the
Friday of the first full week of instruction.
Deadline this quarter is : _____ April 11, 1980

BUSINESS MANAGEMENT
_____
Project Title

Brett Michael Kingstone
_____
Name(s) of student(s): full name & middle initial, nicknames in parentheses

Spring/1980   5
_____
Quarter/Year to be registered   Number of units requested

Professor Paul Griffin   /Grad. School of Bus, 7-3351
_____
Faculty Sponsor (must be Academic Council)   Department   Extension

584 Mayfield Ave. Stanford, CA 94305   /327-8988
_____
Address of student(s), zip code   Telephone

_____/_____

Please provide the following information and return, with this cover sheet and
Faculty Sponsor Statement to the SCIRE office: 590A Old Union. If you are working
with a resource person as well as a faculty sponsor, he or she should also sign a
separate Statement form. Project applications cannot be reviewed until they are
complete. Contact SCIRE staff if you have difficulties (497-4504).

1. A short project description including a brief background to the project.

2. A week-by-week projection of readings, research, fieldwork, meetings with
sponsor, etc. The purpose of this timetable is to encourage you to structure
your work in a coherent way. The ten week outline should demonstrate how you
are structuring your project and how the final product is integral to the
quarter's work. Your outline should give us a good idea of your weekly workload.

3. A description of the final product (paper, journal, etc.) or performance that
will be the basis for evaluation. Describe any other work, written or otherwise,
that will be submitted for evaluation and state the criteria and methods by which
the project will be evaluated.

4. An explanation of how the faculty sponsor will participate in the planning,
guidance, instruction and evaluation of the project.

5. A list of resources (material, people, workshops, interviews, etc.) and an
explanation of how these resources will assist the project. Reading lists should
be detailed; indicate for each item whether it is a book, an article, a pamphlet,
etc., and include the total number of pages to be read from each source. The
amount of reading should also be included in your weekly outline.

6. An explanation of why this project is appropriate for academic credit and why
it should be done through SCIRE rather than through a department.

(over)

Figure 36 – SCIRE Project Application

Getting Credits

If you are enrolled in a special entrepreneurial program, it should be an easy matter for you to get academic credit for running your own business. It may even be part of your course requirement. But even if you are not, it should still be possible for you to get credits, and I recommend that you do so. Those few extra credits may be very important to you one day.

At Stanford, we have a department called SCIRE, the Student Center for Innovative Research and Education, which grants academic credit for student initiated research, internships, productions, and businesses. SCIRE's requirements are that the student obtain a faculty sponsor, submit a project proposal, and turn in a final paper or presentation to be used for evaluating the number of units to be granted, and for grading the project. (See Figure 36.)

If your school does not have a department like SCIRE, you can still seek credits through one of the academic departments such as business, economics, or industrial engineering. Try typing up a well-defined proposal of your "business project" including a statement of time commitments, academic related experience, and work to be submitted for final evaluation. If you discuss your proposal with a few professors in the department and seek their support, you may find this very advantageous when you submit your proposal to the department head.

A Word of Encouragement

Now that you have completed this book you should have a good idea of the necessary steps that you must take in order to start and operate your own part-time small business. It is now up to you to take that first step and start turning your ideas into dollars. You have probably seen many good ideas make other people rich and successful, isn't it time for you to start profiting from your ideas too?

Starting your own business will give you a fresh new perspective of your studies, yourself and possibly your future career. I encourage you to take that first step. You will find it a very profitable and rewarding experience. Who knows? You may build an empire!

Good luck, and go for it!

APPENDIX A

SBA Management Assistance Publications

The Small Business Administration has a series of management assistance publications, all of which are free for the asking. These pamphlets cover a wide range of topics, from tips on borrowing money to reducing air pollution in a small industry, from preventing theft to collecting debts. The Management Aids (MA's) are generally aimed at manufacturing businesses, the Small Marketers Aids (SMA's) at retail and service firms, but there is a good deal of crossover information. There is also a series of bibliographies (SBB's) which give reference sources for particular areas of business. For instance, there are bibliographies on home businesses, on retailing, on advertising, and on recordkeeping systems, to name a few.

Listed below are some of the publications that will be particularly useful for the student entrepreneur. To order any of them, or to get the complete list of available publications, write to the U.S. Small Business Administration, P.O. Box 15434, Fort Worth, TX 76119. You can also order by telephone. The toll free number is 800-433-7212 (in Texas, 800-792-8901).

SMA's

71 Checklist for Going into Business

147 Sound Cash Management and Borrowing

155 Keeping Records in Small Business

163 Public Relations for Small Business

164 Plan Your Advertising Budget

165 Checklist for Profit Watching

MA's

193 What is the Best Selling Price?

194 Marketing Planning Guidelines

200 Is the Independent Sales Agent for You?

205 Pointers on Using Temporary-Help Services

208 Problems in Managing a Family-Owned Business

218 Business Plan for Small Manufacturers

220 Basic Budgets for Profit Planning

224 Association Services for Small Business

225 Management Checklist for a Family Business

230 Selling Products on Consignment

231 Selecting the Legal Structure for Your Business

233 Planning and Goal Setting for Small Business

235 Venture Capital Primer and Small Business

238 Organizing and Staffing a Small Business

SBB's

1 Handicrafts

9 Marketing Research Procedures

10 Retailing

20 Advertising—Retail Store

37 Buying for Retail Stores

72 Personnel Management

86 Training for Small Business

87 Financial Management

90 New Product Development

APPENDIX B

Procedures for Opening Businesses in New York City

Each state, county, and city has its own regulations regarding business taxes and licenses. While the requirements are similar everywhere, specific agency names, forms, licenses, etc., will differ. The best single source of information on what will be required of *your* business is your local Small Business Administration office. (Look in your phone book under United States Government for the SBA listing, or call the Federal Information number if the SBA is not listed there.)

The following material describes the licensing and registration procedures for a business operating in New York City, and lists the required tax forms. These are good examples of the information handouts you can get from SBA. They also illustrate the similarity in regulations in widely separated areas of the United States—the procedures I followed in California were almost identical to those I would have had to comply with in New York.

SCORE
Procedures For Opening a New Business

All new businesses formed in the city are required to follow these procedures:

1. The business should be registered, for applicable business taxes on Form RG 1 at the City Collector's branch office in the borough where the business is located.

2. Make application to the sales Tax Division, State Tax Commission, for a sales tax authorization certificate (St. 105 Certificate of Authority). A resale certificate (St. 120, if required) can also be obtained at the same location.

3. If a tradename or assumed name or partnership is used, Section 440 of the Penal Code requires that it be registered at the County Clerk's office in the county in which the business is located. This blank form can be obtained at a commercial stationery store. (An original and 2 copies should be made up.)

    The registration would not, of course, be required of an incorporated business as same is filed by the Secretary of State.

4. Certain City, State or Federal agencies require special permits for particular types of businesses as follows:

    New York State Dept. of State, Division of Licensing Services, (Licenses Real Estate Brokers, Barbers, Hairdressers, Private Investigators, Cosmetologists, Billiard Rooms, Auto Manufacturers, Steamship Ticket Agents and Notaries).

    New York City Dept. of Consumer Affairs, Division of Licenses, (Licenses Peddlers, Newsstands, Locksmiths, Employment Agencies, Sidewalk Cafes; etc.)

    Foodstore-Restaurant Permits — New York City Dept. of Health, Division of Permit,

    Beer and Alcohol Sales Licensing Applications: Alcoholic Beverage
    Control Board

5. The following government agencies should be consulted if the business will employ workers.

    Unemployment Insurance New York State Division of Employment
    Dept. of Labor

    Labor Regulations (Dealing with hours, minors, minimum wages, etc.)
    New York State Dept. of Labor
    Division of Labor Standards

    Insurance Regulations & Benefits
    Workmen's Compensation Board
    New York State Dept. of Labor

    Social Security Offices

TAX FORMS
For Businesses Operating
in New York City
SOLE PROPRIETORSHIP

Federal

FORM 1040—U.S. Individual Income Tax Return

SCHEDULE C—Profit (or Loss) From Business or Profession

SCHEDULE 1040SE—Computation of Social Security Self-Employment Tax

SCHEDULE 1040ES—Estimated Tax

State & City

FORM IT-201/208—N.Y. State Income Tax Resident Return (plus Form NYC-203 if non-resident of New York City)

FORM IT-2105—Declaration of Estimated Income Tax

FORM IT-202—N.Y. State Unincorporated Business Tax if required)

FORM NYC-202—N.Y. City Unincorporated Business Tax (if required)

PARTNERSHIP
Federal

FORM 1040—U.S. Individual Income Tax Return (for each partner)

FORM 1065—U.S. Partnership Return of Income, plus Schedule K-1—Partners' share of Income, Credits, Deductions, Etc.

FORM 1040ES—Estimated Tax (for each partner)

FORM 1040SE—Computation of Social Security Self-Employment Tax (for each partner)

State & City

FORM IT-204—N.Y. State Partnership Return

FORM IT-201/208—N.Y. State Income Tax Resident Return (for each partner (plus Form NYC-203 if non-resident of New York City)

FORM IT-2105—N.Y. State Declaration of Estimated Tax (for each partner)

FORM NYC-202—City of New York Unincorporated Business Tax (if required)

CORPORATION
Federal

FORM 1120—U.S. Corporation Income Tax Return

FORM 503—U.S. Corporation Estimated Tax Deposit Form

*FORM 941—Federal Income Tax Withholding Tax

*FORM 501—Federal Tax Deposit Form for Withholding & Federal Insurance Contributions Act Taxes (FICA)

*FORM 940—Federal Unemployment Tax Act Taxes (FUTA)

*FORM 508—Quarterly Deposits of Actual FUTA Liability (only if in excess of $100)

State & City

FORMS CT-3 or CT-4—N.Y. State Corporation Franchise Tax Report

FORMS NYC-3L or NYC-4S—N.Y. City General Corporation Tax Return

*Also required from Sole Proprietorships and Partnerships with one or more employees.

Bibliography

Your development as an entrepreneur should not end with this book! Here is a list of magazines and books that will give you added information and may broaden your creative horizons. Most of them can be found at your local school library. The more specialized works can be found in business school libraries or you can contact the publishers directly.

Magazines and Periodicals

Barrons National Business and Financial Weekly
22 Cortlandt St.
New York, NY 10007

Business Week
McGraw-Hill, Inc.
1221 Ave. of the Americas
New York, NY 10020

Entrepreneurs' Magazine
2311 Pontius Ave.
Los Angeles, CA 90064

Forbes
60 Fifth Ave.
New York, NY 10011

Fortune
Time/Life Building
New York, NY 10020

Nations Business
1615 H St. NW
Washington, D.C. 20062

Venture Magazine
35 W. 45th St.
New York, NY 10036

Wall Street Journal
22 Courtlandt St.
New York, NY 10007

Books

Allen, Louis. *Starting and Succeeding in Your Own Small Business.* Grosset and Dunlap, 1960.

Ballas, George, and Hollas, Dave. *The Making of an Entrepreneur: Keys to Your Success.* Prentice-Hall, 1980.

Baumback, Clifford, and Lawyer, Kenneth. *How to Organize and Operate a Small Business.* Prentice-Hall, 1973.

Briarpatch. *Briarpatch Book: Experiences in Right Livelihood and Simple Living.* Reed Books, 1978.

Burstinger, Irving. *The Small Business Handbook: Comprehensive Guide to Starting and Running Your Own Business.* Spectrum Books, 1979.

Danco, Leon. *Beyond Survival: A Business Owner's Guide for Success.* Reston Publishing Company, 1975.

Dible, Donald. *Up Your Own Organization: A Handbook for the Employed, the Unemployed, and the Self-Employed on How to Start and Finance a New Business.* The Entrepreneur Press, 1974.

Drucker, Peter F. *Management: Tasks, Practices, Responsibilities.* Harper and Row, 1974.

Feinman, Jeffrey. *One Hundred Surefire Businesses You Can Start with Little or No Investment.* Playboy Press, 1976.

Friedman, Milton. *Capitalism and Freedom.* University of Chicago Press, 1962.

Friedman, Milton, and Friedman, Rose. *Free to Choose: A Personal Statement.* Harcourt Brace Jovanovich, Inc., 1980.

Hill, Napoleon. *Think and Grow Rich.* Fawcett Crest Books, 1960.

Hoge, Cecil. *Mail Order Moonlighting.* Ten Speed Press, 1976.

Kamoroff, Bernard. *Small Time Operator: How to Start Your Own Small Business, Keep Your Books, Pay Your Taxes, and Stay Out of Trouble*. Bell Springs Press, 1974.

Klatt, Lawrence. *Small Business Management: Essentials for Entrepreneurship*. Wadsworth Publishing Co., 1973.

Kracke, Don and Honkanen, Roger. *How to Turn Your Idea into a Million Dollars*. Mentor Books, 1979.

Lasser, Jacob. K. *How to Run a Small Business*. McGraw-Hill, 1979.

McCaslin, Barbara S., and McNamara, Patricia P. *Be Your Own Boss: A Woman's Guide to Planning and Running Her Own Business*. Prentice-Hall, 1980.

Phillips, Michael, et al. *Seven Laws of Money*. Random House, 1974.

Rand, Ayn. *Atlas Shrugged*. Random House, 1957.

Shook, Robert L. *The Entrepreneurs: Twelve Who Took Risks and Succeeded*. Harper and Row, 1980.

Simon, William E. *A Time for Truth*. Reader's Digest Press, 1978.

Vesper, Karl. *Entrepreneurship Education*. Available from Babson College, Wellesley, MA 02157. 1976.

Vesper, Karl. *New Venture Strategies*. Prentice-Hall, 1980.

Winston, Sandra. *The Entrepreneurial Woman*. Bantam Books, 1980.

The American Association of Entrepreneurs

Registered in the County of Santa Clara, California

P.O. Box 5771
Stanford, CA 94305

Director:
Brett Johnson

Chairman:
Brett Kingstone

Advisors:
Jamie Halper
Tony Robbins
Steve Wilson

Join the American Association of Entrepreneurs. Your membership fee entitles you to a membership card and a national directory of entrepreneurs across the country which will be published in January. The membership will be renewable annually and the Entrepreneur's Directory will be revised each January. The American Association of Entrepreneurs is dedicated to bringing entrepreneurs and their ideas from all over the country closer together. We believe this association will aid entrepreneurs in establishing contacts across the country which will undoubtedly lead to new ventures. We encourage you to send us your thoughts and ideas in helping us develop our association.

Please list your name, address, phone number and current business or business plan on the form below and mail it to the above address with an enclosed check for seven dollars made out to the American Association of Entrepreneurs. You may also enclose additional information about your business or business idea which may be used in future newsletters. Pictures should be black and white glossies.

Name: _____

Address: _____

Phone Number:　Home: _____　Office: _____

Current Business or Entrepreneurial Plans _____

_____

_____

_____

_____